For the magic of Eric

ORO Editions
Publishers of Architecture, Art, and Design
Gordon Goff: Publisher
Managing Editor: Jake Anderson

www.oroeditions.com
info@oroeditions.com

Published by ORO Editions

Author: Leslie Van Duzer
Book Design: Pablo Mandel / circularstudio.com

Typeset in TT Norms and Minion

10 9 8 7 6 5 4 3 2 1 First Edition

ISBN: 978-1-951541-77-4

Color Separations and Printing: ORO Group Ltd.
Printed in China.

ORO Editions makes a continuous effort to minimize the overall carbon footprint of its publications. As part of this goal, ORO Editions, in association with Global ReLeaf, arranges to plant trees to replace those used in the manufacturing of the paper produced for its books. Global ReLeaf is an international campaign run by American Forests, one of the world's oldest nonprofit conservation organizations. Global ReLeaf is American Forests' education and action program that helps individuals, organizations, agencies, and corporations improve the local and global environment by planting and caring for trees.

ALMOST, NOT

THE ARCHITECTURE OF ATELIER NISHIKATA

LESLIE VAN DUZER

ORO Editions – Novato, California

CONTENTS

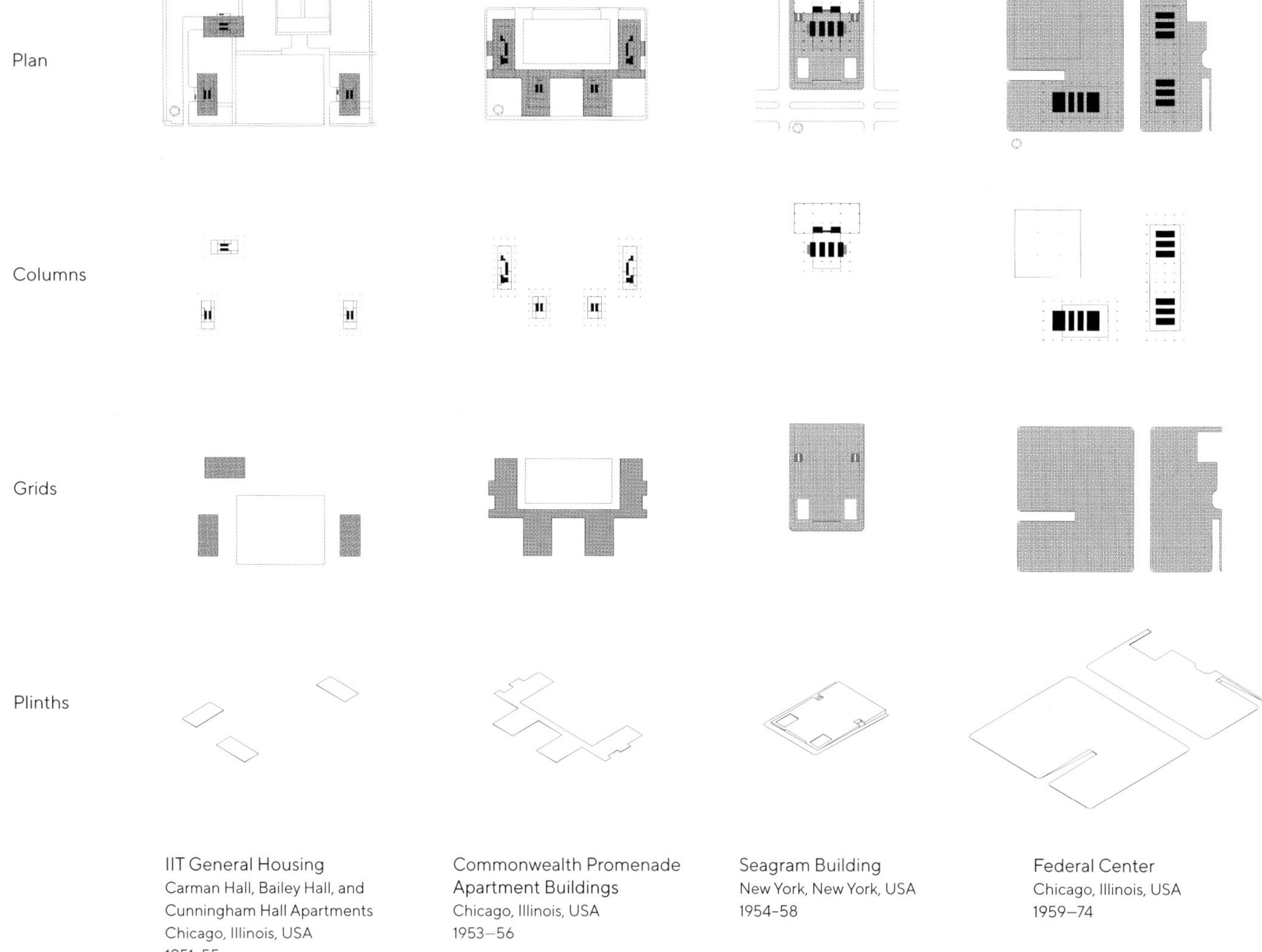

IIT General Housing
Carman Hall, Bailey Hall, and Cunningham Hall Apartments
Chicago, Illinois, USA
1951–55

Commonwealth Promenade Apartment Buildings
Chicago, Illinois, USA
1953–56

Seagram Building
New York, New York, USA
1954–58

Federal Center
Chicago, Illinois, USA
1959–74

ALMOST, NOT

"The hallucinatory effect derives from the extraordinary
clarity and not from mystery or mist.
Nothing is more fantastic ultimately than precision."

Alain Robbe-Grillet

On any given day, the proponents of this story, partners Reiko Nishio and Hirohito Ono, can be found in the Tokyo neighborhood of Nishikata pursuing their vocation with the intensity of monks. When they are not occupied with commissioned work, they are exploring ideas through unbuilt projects. When they are not designing, they are teaching, or studying architecture themselves. Most recently they have measured and drawn the column, podium and paving grid typologies in Mies van der Rohe's North American buildings. It is not the profession of architecture, with all its attendant trappings, that interests these architects, but rather the discipline itself.

This volume presents four built works by Atelier Nishikata, a practice established by Nishio and Ono in 2000. The projects, all modest in scale and budget, all in or near Tokyo, include: the conversion of a single-family house for three into a triplex for seven; the joining of two penthouse units when a family of six became four; the conversion of a four-room apartment into five rooms, or maybe ten; and an eight-level infill house for one.

Until now, this body of work has not received much exposure outside of Japan. As all the projects are private residences, none of the interiors are accessible to the public. Additionally, the experiential complexity of the work challenges the limits of photography and its originality defies searchable descriptors. Indeed, the architecture of Atelier Nishikata is elusive, actively resisting capture and consumption. It is more timeless than of its time.

This durability may be attributed to the architects' core aspiration: the creation of poetic images in which "inhabited space transcends geometrical space."[1] In their practice, architecture is understood to be capable of masking its own material presence, just as a magician's requisite props are hidden in the midst of an illusion. Architecture transcends its physical boundaries and its visual image when it fully engages the body and its spatial imagination.

1. Gaston Bachelard, *The Poetics of Space*, trans. Maria Jolas (Boston: Beacon Press, 1969), 47.

Magicians have much in common with our architects, sharing both their aspirations and their techniques. The late magician and scholar Ricky Jay stated: "Magic is all about structure. You have to take the observer from the ordinary, to the extraordinary, to the astounding."[2] Borrowing from magic parlance, both the magician and the architects begin with *The Pledge*, the presentation and affirmation of something quotidian: a coin or a column. Only after they have established the ordinary nature of their props can they produce the extraordinary. In *The Turn*, when the magician vanishes a coin into thin air and the architect opens a small door on the front of a column revealing a closet, they force a startling confrontation with our preconceptions. But it is the finale, *The Prestige*, that evokes true astonishment. The same coin, signed by the audience member during *The Pledge* and vanished in *The Turn*, miraculously reappears in the volunteer's pocket, doubling the climax. Likewise, when a second door in the column opens unexpectedly, transforming the column-turned-closet into a column-turned-window, our bewilderment multiplies. In their work, Atelier Nishikata invites us to reconsider not only the function of a column, but also the very definition of a picture window, a vaulted ceiling, a door and so much more. Over and over again, these architects, like their theatrical counterparts, acknowledge our assumptions by upending them. Normal becomes *almost*-normal.

Many masters have played at this game. Artist Walter Pichler's *almost*-vernacular farmhouses in the Austrian countryside are, upon closer inspection, meticulously detailed, sacred shelters for his fragile figures. Gunnar Asplund's Villa Snellman and its *almost*-classical facade presents not one but two front doors and windows ever-so-slightly adrift off center. Then consider Mies's *almost*-modern, so-called "brick villas" in Krefeld, with their brick veneers disguising massive steel structures. In each case, assumptions are *almost* affirmed, but then they aren't. Farmhouse? Not. Classical symmetry? Not quite. Brick structure? Not even close.

In such encounters, when one is confronted with the distance between what one experiences in the moment and what one remembers, between what is perceived and what "should" be, one's continuity of confidence is disrupted. This confrontation with the *almost*- triggers a delightfully destabilizing oscillation between certainty and uncertainty, curiosity and astonishment, past and present experience, delaying any automated consumption.

The *almost*-ordinary character of Atelier Nishikata's work, engendered by the use of common materials—plywood and gypsum board, wallpaper and white paint—and familiar architectural elements—gables and vaults, sliding screens and pocket doors—belies complex internal dialogues that unfold through direct physical engagement. Golden ratio proportioned windows, ergonomically perfect footrests, barely passable passageways, unusually steep stairs, all give scale to the body. Abnormal systems for shuttering windows and opening doors require a recalibration of learned movements. Labyrinthine spatial sequences and phenomenal transparencies create a keen awareness of the body's position in space. The mind is busy

2. Tom Zito, "Appreciation: The Pledge. The Turn. The Prestige," *Alta Online*, December 18, 2018, https://altaonline.com/the-pledge-the-turn-the-prestige/.

1. Compound, Burgenland
Walter Pichler
Photo: Niki.L / CC BY-SA

2. Villa Snellman, Djursholm
Gunnar Asplund
Photo: Marc Treib

3. Haus Lange, Krefeld
Ludwig Mies van der Rohe
Kunstmuseum Krefeld
Photo: Volker Döhne

1

2

3

remembering the present and forgetting the future as the architecture quite literally alters one's sense of time. The experience is an invigorating, full-body workout.

Atelier Nishikata operates with great precision, deploying a limited palette of techniques strategically and methodically, over and over again. First, rules are established, each with their own internal logic. The rules are then layered, one atop another, and another, producing intentional misalignments. Second, repetition variation involves creating recurring elements to establish relationships between noncontiguous spaces. Variables are then introduced to differentiate and add complexity. Finally, category jumping allows the architects to breathe new life into common architectural components.

By simultaneously operating on many levels, the architecture of Atelier Nishikata enables the "fourth dimension…the moment of limitless escape."[3] In his essay "Ineffable Space," Le Corbusier continues: "In a complete and successful work there are hidden masses of implications, a veritable world which reveals itself to those whom it may concern, which means: to those who deserve it. Then a boundless depth opens up, effaces the walls, drives away contingent presences, accomplishes the miracle of ineffable space." It is safe to say the architecture of Atelier Nishikata is only for those whom it may concern.

EFFECT: DELAY
TECHNIQUE: LAYERED RULES

For each new project, the architects establish multiple rules. These have different informants—geometry, ergonomics, context, program—varying from project to project. There are rules for the dimensions of floor plans, the size and position of windows, the type of doors, the joints in the cladding, the pattern in the flooring and so on. These independent systems are then layered over one another, and in the case of renovations, over the existing conditions.

Within any given rule, they allow for exceptions. These rogue elements are most clearly evident in House in Awaji where nearly every rule established is broken, upending even the most astute visitor's attempt to unpack the work. Just when one thinks they have deciphered the rules for the distribution of public and private spaces, or the dispersal of windows, or the orientation of the vaults, a single deviant sends the head spinning.

While it is not unusual in the design process to establish rules for different components, what is highly unusual is the intentional lack of resolution between them. In the architecture of Atelier Nishikata, headers of windows and doors unconventionally resist alignment. Horizontal bands of wallpaper designed to encircle and frame a room are unapologetically disrupted by door and window frames. One square room even marks two different centers based on two different sets of conflicting geometries. These autonomous logics and their collective

3. Le Corbusier, *New World of Space* (New York: Reynal & Hitchcock, 1948), 8.

misalignments are certainly not the result of miscalculation or poor craft, but rather, a very intentional strategy.

These incoincident layers produce a compounding, confounding effect comparable to being caught between crossing conversations at a dinner party or being subjected to a magician's multiple distractions. Just as it is nearly impossible to eavesdrop on several dialogues at once or to reconcile a magician's patter and busy hands, so too it is challenging at best to disentangle formal logics intentionally entangled. Forced to shift attention from one thing to another, one simply cannot grasp the whole, whether it is an accurate transcript of the dinner conversation, a full understanding of the magician's ploys or a comprehensive, concrete image of this architecture.

In the work of Atelier Nishikata, the intentional dissonance between architectural components forces a delay in comprehension and consumption, forestalling any easy confirmation of readymade assumptions. By establishing the formal autonomy of each component—whether a door or a skylight—the architects create a robust internal architectural dialogue which allows for ever-changing programs, which in turn defines an enviable durability.

EFFECT: DÉJÀ VU
TECHNIQUE: REPETITION VARIATION

The lucky among us will experience at least once in a lifetime that sudden, startling sense of familiarity during a first-time encounter, that is, déjà vu or already seen. This is a false memory, a discrepant event. Some associate déjà vu with the past, with reincarnation or preexistence; others consider it a form of reading the future, of precognition. While there appears to be no consensus, the defining characteristic of déjà vu is the simultaneous occupation of multiple timeframes: present-past or present-future.

While there may be other methods for intentionally conjuring the experience of déjà vu, what Alfred Tennyson referred to in an early sonnet as "states of mystical similitude," Atelier Nishikata uses a strategy well-worn in advertising: *repetition variation*. This technique is designed to reinforce a message while minimizing consumer wearout. Any number of ad campaigns could be cited as examples, but consider Apple's successful *Think Different* campaign that ran for five years, from 1997–2002. In every ad, three features remained constant: a black-and-white portrait of a celebrity, the Apple logo and the grammatically challenged, catchy slogan: "Think Different." To ensure engagement, personalities with a wide range of accomplishments, from Rosa Parks to Albert Einstein, provided content-rich variation.

Of course the effective use of repetition variation, or difference and sameness, can be found in all creative disciplines. To mention just a few examples from art: Sol LeWitt's cubes, Donald Judd's progressions, Andy Warhol's silkscreens ("you get the same image, slightly different

4

5

6

4. WOZOCO, Amsterdam
MVRDV
Photo: Ron 't Hart

5. Housing Schönwilpark Meggen
Diener & Diener Architekten
Photo: Yohan Zerdoun

6. Kunstmuseum Appenzell
Gigon/Guyer Architects
Photo: Gaston Wicky

each time"),[4] Josef Albers minimalist squares and Becher and Becher's industrial typologies ("a more or less perfect chain of serial rhythms and repetitions").[5]

As nearly all buildings are designed with repetitive structural members and program areas, fixtures and apertures, architecture is inherently well positioned to employ repetition variation as a means to evolve new types. The 1960s spawned an international proliferation of projects that exposed and exploited these fundamental aspects of architecture in both built and unbuilt projects. Consider just a few that played with units and variegated multiples: the Metabolists in Tokyo, Archigram in London, Aldo van Eyck in Amsterdam, Moshie Safdie in Montreal. More recently, repetition variation has been used to activate facades of office and apartment buildings by interrupting uniform fenestration patterns, from the extreme scramble of MVRDV's WOZOCO housing to the subtle, almost musical variations composed by Diener and Diener. The spatial progression in Gigon and Guyer's Kunstmuseum Appenzell, with its resulting effect of déjà vu (I think I have already been in this gallery, but then again, I have not seen that window before), comes close to Atelier Nishikata's application of this technique.

Nishio and Ono take inspiration from sources both inside and outside their discipline. Their aforementioned, patient study of Mies's repetitive but contextually varied typologies has been instructive, as has Adolf Loos's unabashed repetition of program-affiliated spatial configurations. Repetition variation in film has been another significant influence, with a specific mention of Yasujirō Ozu's frames in *Tokyo Story* and Roberto Rossellini's doors in *Rome, Open City.*

At the start of every project, Atelier Nishikata introduces a degree of sameness. In the case of their renovations, this order is imposed on dissimilar spaces. The architects might decide to repeat a square plan, or a centered column, or a vaulted ceiling. Once they have created a relationship between generally noncontiguous spaces by establishing sameness, difference is introduced. The dimensions of the square plans might vary. The interior of one centered column might be accessible, while another one not. A vaulted ceiling might be oriented this way in one space and that way in another. Importantly, no two rooms are ever identical.

What is of utmost importance to the architects are the relationships between spaces. While architecture, like film, unfolds in linear time, making it impossible to simultaneously occupy two frames or two spaces at once, in each present moment, the use of repetition variation causes one to recall the past and anticipate the future. It is in this way that the architecture of Atelier Nishikata exceeds its physical limitations.

4. Andy Warhol and Pat Hackett, *POPism: The Warhol Sixties* (New York: Harcourt Brace Jovanovich, 1980), 22.

5. Blake Stimson, "The Photographic Comportment of Bernd and Hilla Becher," *Tate Papers,* Tate, Spring 2004, https://www.tate.org.uk/research/publications/tate-papers/01/photographic-comportment-of-bernd-and-hilla-becher.

EFFECT: DETOUR

TECHNIQUE: CATEGORY JUMPING

Psychologist Jean Piaget proposed that there are two ways of processing new information and experiences. The first is through *assimilation* where new knowledge is filed into existing mental categories, or schemas. The second, of particular interest here, is the more difficult *accommodation* which requires reshaping an existing category, or in some cases creating a wholly new category to accommodate unfamiliar information.

Here, the art of magic is again instructive. At the start of an effective illusion, the magician first assists the audience in *assimilating* his prop into a familiar category. In the *Pencil through Coin* trick, s/he commits much patter to convincing the audience that the coin is authentic before magically penetrating its center with a pencil. The magician repeatedly names the coin, conjuring up common coin schemas. S/he taps the coin on the tabletop to prove its rigidity and passes it around for confirmation, ensuring that the audience files the coin into the mental category *solid things.* Magic essentially involves moving something from one category to another, in this case, a coin from *solid things* to *permeable things,* forcing the audience to *accommodate* the coin in a new category. This forced accommodation is what bewilders.

As one routinely files a coin away in multiple categories—*solid things, things in a pocket, things found in multiples* or *things in a bank*—the magician can choose which category to stretch. S/he considers, among other possibilities, whether altering the object's material, scale, quantity and/or context will be most effective.

In the *Pencil through Coin* trick, the illusion involves (apparently) changing the material quality of the coin. In another material transformation, the classic *Indian Rope* trick, a rope is shown limp before it stiffens to allow a child to climb it as a pole. Rope has been moved from the category *limp things* (which also contains cooked spaghetti) to *stiff things* (along with starched collars). Beyond material transformations, the magician has other tricks up her/his sleeve.

A change in scale can play an important role, as when a grown assistant appears from a small box. The body has moved from the category *things the size of a coffin* to *things that fit in small containers.* Likewise, when a magician pulls a very long streamer from her/his mouth, the streamers have moved from *things that can span a room* (like a shout or steel beams) to *things that fit in a mouth* (like dentures or a raisin).

The magician challenges our expectations around quantity when s/he pours liquid from a large container into a smaller container with no overflow. Here, a categorical leap is made from *containers with finite volume* to the oxymoronic category *containers with infinite volume.* Often quantity, material and scale work together, for example, when the magician pulls no less than ten (quantity) fragile eggs (material) from a coat pocket (scale).

A change in context is another challenge to rigid mental frameworks. When an elephant appears on stage, the magician has moved the beast from the category *wild animals* to the category *animal actors.* The dislocation of an elephant from the wild, or even from the zoo, to a magic theater is schema shattering. And when the elephant later vanishes into thin air, moving from *things that weigh tons* to *things that blow away,* it joins the good company of wispy clouds and dandelion fluff.

Artists have long played the game of estrangement by category jumping. By moving a urinal from the category *things found in a bathroom* to *things found in an art gallery,* Marcel Duchamp changed the course of 20th art with *Fountain.* In *Bicycle Wheel,* he moved the wheel from one category to another when he mounted it atop a stool, from *things that spin to propel* (like tires) to *things that spin in place* (like pinwheels or a potter's wheel). Countless artists followed Duchamp's lead. In *Bang* Ai Wei Wei levitated 886 stools, shifting them from *things to sit on* to *things that are suspended.* Tobias Wong transferred Alvar Aalto's iconic vase from *things that are fragile* to *things that are durable* when he filled the expensive vase with concrete, (apparently) smashed the glass and named the new object *Doorstop.* And on and on.

In the architecture of Atelier Nishikata, architectural components are interrogated for their potential transformation. As alchemists turn stone to gold, Atelier Nishikata transforms architecture's everyday components into rarified objects that challenge well-established object schemas. What is a column when it contains a closet, when it has been moved from the category *things that support* (grouped with scaffolding and good friends) to the category *things that support and contain* (like bras and hammocks)? Is a closet without a back, a thick threshold one passes through, still a closet? What is a picture window that opens onto a neighbor's wall half a meter away? Is it still called roofing paper when it blankets a facade?

The architecture of Atelier Nishikata does not allow for easy assimilation, but rather requires accommodation, either the expansion of existing categories, or in some cases, the invention of new ones. This accommodation is precisely how new types are borne.

In closing, it is useful to quote Rafael Moneo at length: "Types are transformed—that is, one type becomes another, when substantial elements in the formal structure are changed. ...In this continuous process of transformation, the architect can extrapolate from the type, changing its use; he can distort the type by means of a transformation of scale; he can overlap different types to produce new ones. He can use formal quotations of a known type in a different context, as well as create new types by a radical change in the techniques already employed. The list of different mechanisms is extensive—it is a function of the inventiveness of architects."[6]

6. Rafael Moneo, "On Typology," *Oppositions* 13 (Summer 1978): 24, 27.

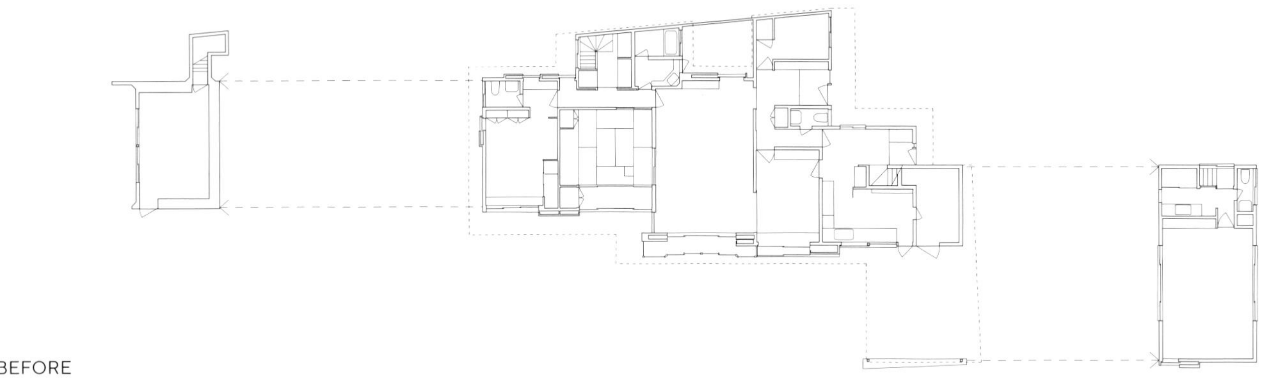
BEFORE

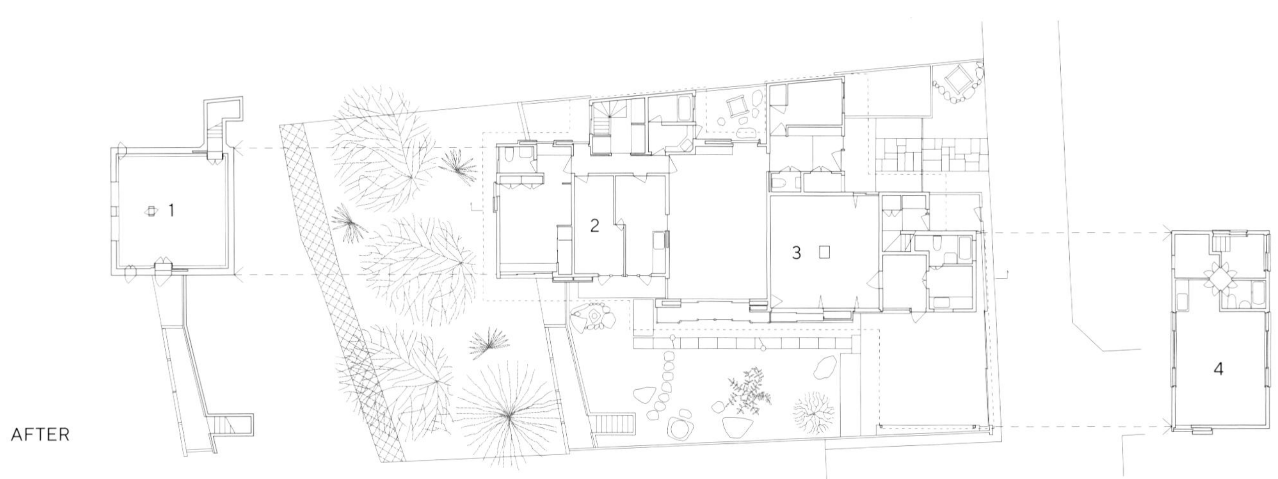

AFTER

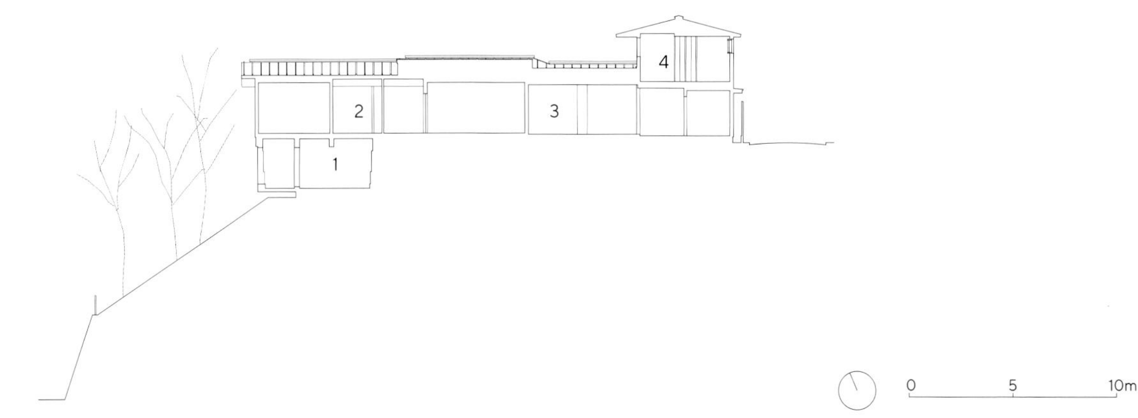

FOUR EPISODES

Four Episodes is the remarkable renovation of an unremarkable house on a quiet street in Bunkyo, Tokyo. This story began with a recognition by the inhabitants—grandmother, mother and adult son—that the sprawling layout of the house and the cost of maintaining excess space were not sustainable. With the mother advancing in age herself, and the care of her elderly mother ongoing, the family decided to shrink their living quarters and create two new rental apartments. In 2009, Atelier Nishikata was engaged to convert the single-family house into a triplex.

The renovation would consist of four episodes, phased to allow the residents to remain in the house throughout the construction. Episode One: The dark and dank basement, suitable only for storage, would be enlarged and illuminated to create a retreat from the main living spaces. The room was envisioned as a gallery for the mother, a painter, or as a semi-autonomous living space for her son. Episode Two: Under the circumstances, the traditional tatami room was no longer practical. The large, centrally located space would be divided in half to create a guest room for visiting relatives and a new, more conveniently located kitchen. Episode Three: The new kitchen would free up the original kitchen and dining room for the first rental apartment. Episode Four: The only second-story space, a vaulted room with generous windows overlooking the street and the garden, would be converted into an additional, income-generating unit. In 2011, the Great East Japan Earthquake added urgency to the project and a new requirement: a seismic upgrade.

As the four episodes are noncontiguous, the architects introduced two architectural motifs to establish a relationship between the spaces. Inspired by the underlying, traditional geometry of the house, they determined that each space would be square and the center of each space would be marked by a column.

While most would pass by this 1960s house without a second glance, the observant among them would notice something amiss. Villa Snellman and Haus Lange notwithstanding, it is odd for a single-family house to have two front doors, or more specifically in this case, two front gates leading to two distinct entry courts. And if per chance the sliding gate securing the carport happens to be open, the passerby might catch a glimpse of a third "front" door. But it would take a determined trespasser with insider's knowledge to venture into the carport, through the long overgrown garden, down a flight of stairs, and along a narrow footpath on the very edge of the Hongo Plateau to find the fourth entry. But here is where the story of Four Episodes begins.

I White Room

The garden path culminates at the White Room. The facade of this basement space, half buried, half exposed, is differentiated from the rest of the house by a white plaster finish, with stripes of alternating textures, and apertures framed in lipstick-red. The two glazed openings invite a peek, but unexpectedly, deny a view. Contrary to expectations, the small window reveals nothing but an empty cabinet, and the glass door, just an empty closet reminiscent of an Yves Klein *Void Room*.

To enter the White Room from the garden, the first of two possible entries into the space, requires an elaborate, five-step operation: swing open the glass door, slide aside a screened panel, walk across the empty closet-threshold, push through the double doors, and step down into the space.

VOLUME AND LIGHT

The west wall of the original basement was demolished and the space extended to form the first of the four square rooms. Two new picture windows facing west and two smaller windows on opposing walls facing north and south transform the space, providing welcome illumination and views to a grove of deciduous trees. The composition of the two picture windows and a small section of wall between them conforms to the golden ratio, while the proportions of the two smaller apertures are taken from a window in Taian, a traditional tea house in Kyoto.

BEAMS

A structural beam commemorates the vanquished wall, enriching the reflected ceiling plan and adding complexity to the reading of the space. In collaboration with a second beam, the two divide the new space roughly in thirds, the square space becoming three rectangular spaces oriented north-south. The westernmost rectangle contains the four windows, the middle section, the closet-window-door to the garden, and the final rear third, the closet-door to the stairs joining the basement to the ground-floor living spaces.

COLUMN

A new column provides structural stability while accomplishing so much more. Centered on the north-south axis, it further complicates the reading of the space as three rectangles by effectively dividing the room into 1/3-2/3, separating the westernmost space from the other

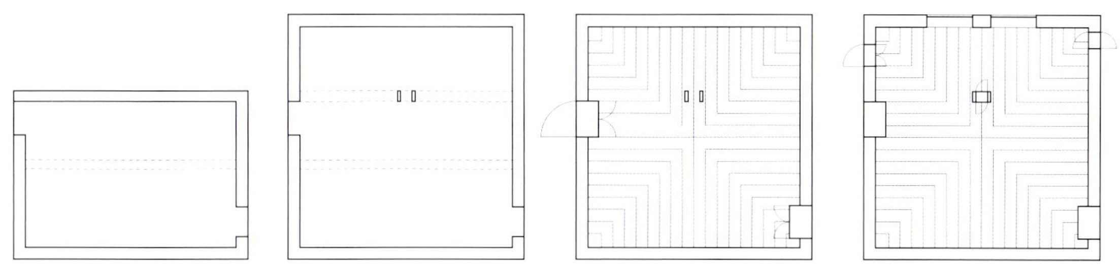

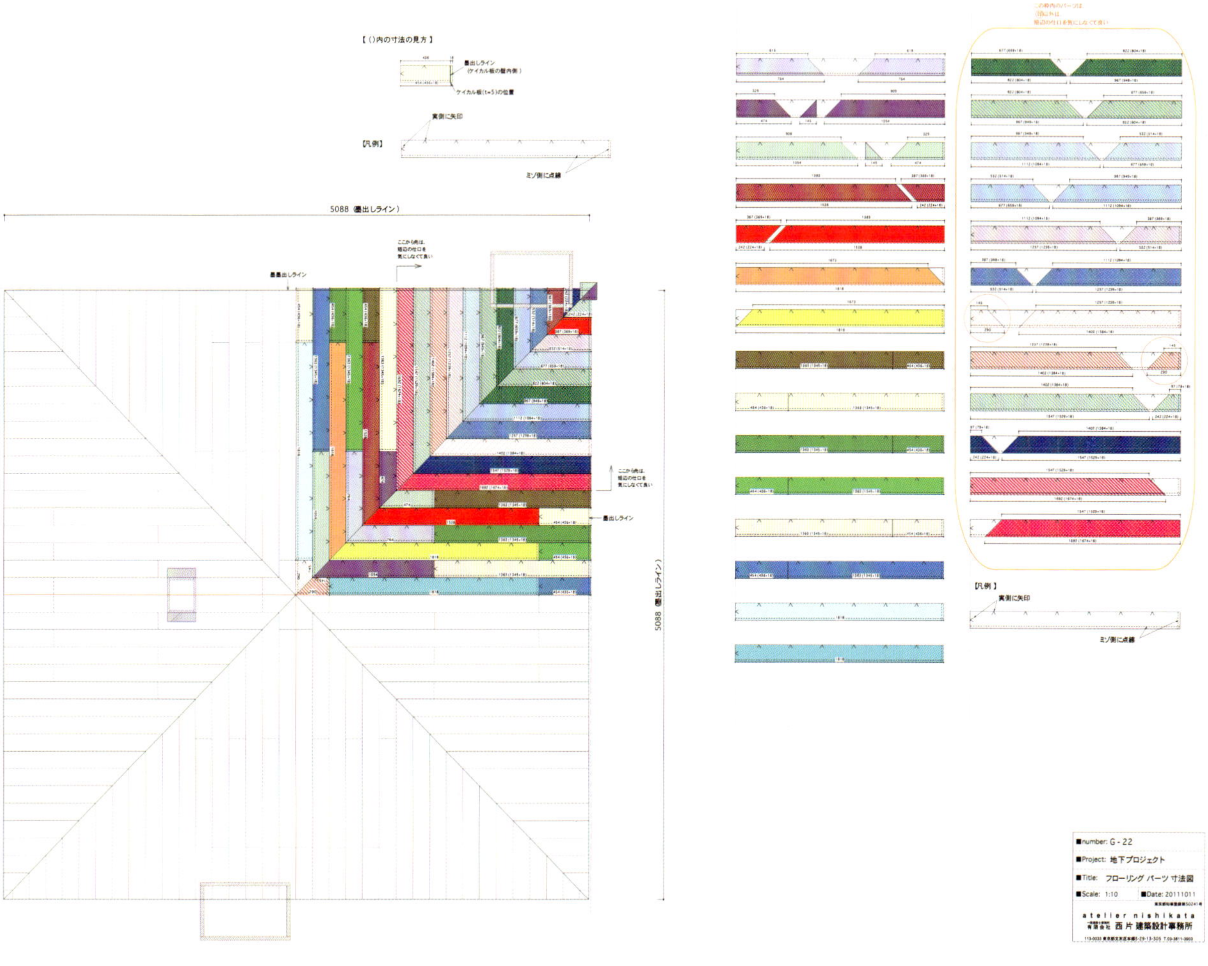

【()内の寸法の見方】

墨出しライン

【凡例】

実側に矢印

ミゾ側に点線

5088（墨出しライン）

■number: G - 22

■Project: 地下プロジェクト

■Title: フローリング パーツ 寸法図

■Scale: 1:10 ■Date: 20111011

atelier nishikata

有限会社 西片建築設計事務所

Working drawing for flooring

two. Performing double duty, it also divides the square in half along the east-west axis. Between the two beams and the column, the room has effectively been divided into numerous subspaces with ill-defined boundaries. With phenomenal spatial transparencies constantly in flux, the spaces cannot be easily enumerated.

This resulting spatial complexity allows for multiple readings, providing useful flexibility for the inhabitants. The White Room could be a beautiful gallery, or it could be an endlessly adaptable living space with a couch in one corner defining a living room, a desk hugging the centered column, a study, and so on.

One of the most important roles for the column, aside from providing structural support and dividing the space productively, is impeding any possible view of the entire room. With some portion of the room always obscured by the column, the spatial imagination remains engaged.

FLOORING

The new floorboards are laid in a diagonal pattern emanating from the four corners. The resulting X establishes spatial stability by marking the true geometric center of the square room. The stasis created by the pattern in the floor, with its strong diagonal lines and emphatic centerpoint, coexists in palatable tension with the dynamic and amorphous spatial transparencies engendered by the beams and column. This discordant dialogue is just one of many that can be heard in the White Room.

CLOSETED APERTURES

The spatial relationship between the two (apparently) identical door-closets cuts diagonally across two of the three rectangles, dividing overlapping orthogonal spaces and defying the will of the floorboards for stability. The diagonal, a desire line or shortcut from entry to exit, is inevitably interrupted when the space is fully furnished.

The two portals into the basement were maintained in their original positions, but their ordinary swing doors were replaced with complicated constellations of components. To reach the stair leading to the upper level of the house requires another elaborate sequence, similar but not identical to the garden entry. Pull open the two narrow doors and step up into a closet. A bare bulb hangs from the ceiling, but one searches in vain for any means to hang clothes. Channeling Lucy from the *Chronicles of Narnia*, slide open the back of the closet, and climb into the next episode.

The opening of the two small windows also requires a series of unfamiliar moves: open the flush cabinet door(s), pull the recessed screen panel inward and push out the red window frames. The swing-and-slide moves required to open and close the windows and doors in the White Room confirm that these four void spaces are intent on remaining empty.

Further confounding the spatial complexity of the White Room, the already productive column is closeted too. On its east and west sides, there are narrow doors. When one door is open, the column becomes a tall, narrow cabinet fit for umbrellas or a broom. When both doors

are open, the remaining structure frames views of two opposing walls. And if the inhabitant is broom-thin, the column additionally provides passage between spaces. With the opening and closing of the five door-, window- and column-closets, the perception of space in the White Room is continually transforming.

CLADDING

As the beams and column, apertures and floorboards, engage in dynamic dialogues that criss-cross the space, the walls are arguing among themselves. The floor-to-ceiling cladding follows two conflicting rules: one for the horizontal ledges and one for the vertical seams.

Stepped back in section, the horizontal ledges ring the room at three heights, each driven by human proportions. The lowest ledge is an ideal footrest, the middle ledge, a perfect place to set a cup of tea. By positioning the uppermost ledge with its top surface well above eye level and out of convenient reach, the architects create the illusion of a higher ceiling. Between the three shallow ledges, there is subtle variation in the wall surface. The middle section, constructed of plywood and painted with a glossy finish, serves as a pin-up surface; the upper and lower sections are covered with plasterboard and finished with a matte paint.

While the three ledges encircle the room reinforcing its integrity, the vertical joints, determined by an entirely different logic, disrupt the continuity of the horizontal lines. The rhythm of the vertical joints, established by the window-wall composition on the western elevation, is repeated verbatim on the other three elevations without the slightest regard for the location of beams or windows or doors. Clear-eyed intent is evident as misalignments abound; indeed, the conflict between the horizontal ledges and the vertical joints serves as an intentional distraction from the lure of the seductive western view.

By now one's body has been twisted into knots trying to eavesdrop on a multitude of overlapping conversations. The turn-right, turn-left, look-up, look-down experience of being in a space so confounding, so illegible, brings the inhabitant into an engaging and energetic relationship with the architecture. And if a second person enters the room, and the two inhabitants exchange both with one another and with the architecture, evermore complex relationships abound.

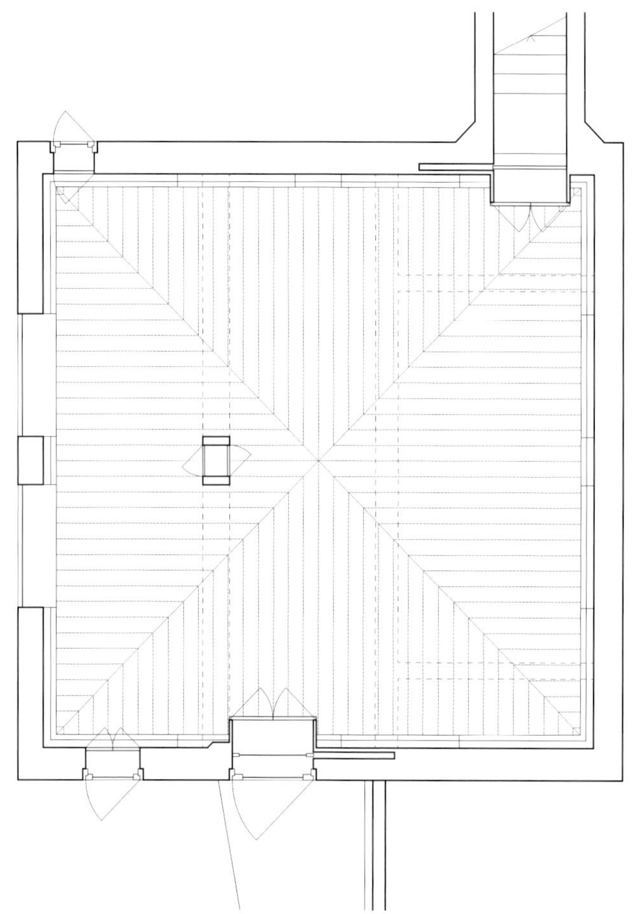

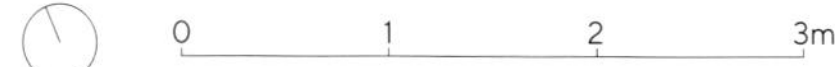
0
1
2
3m

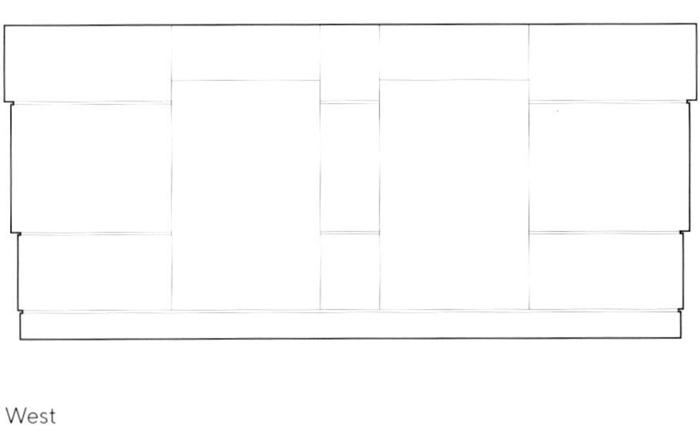

West

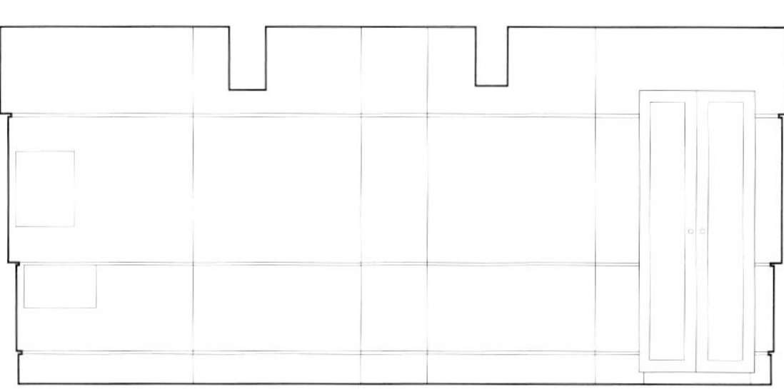

North

East

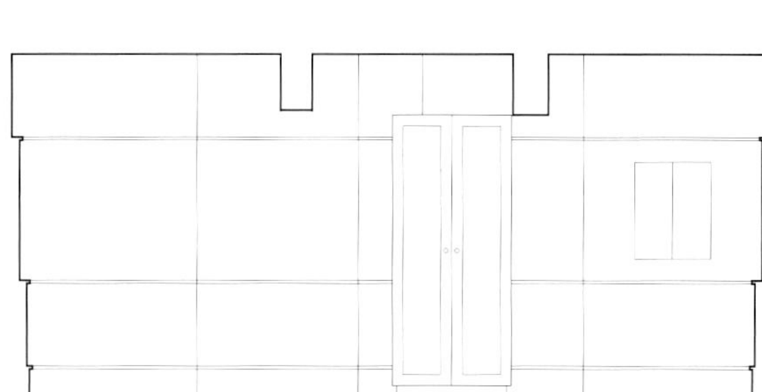

South

0 1 2 3m

II Moto-Washitsu

Episode Two unfolds on the main floor of the house, adjacent to the central living room, in the *moto-washitsu,* or former traditional room. The interior fittings of the square room—the eight tatami mats, alcove, *engawa* (veranda), *shoji* and *fusuma* (translucent and opaque sliding screens)—were removed in order to create two rooms from the space of one: a new guest bedroom and a kitchen.

WALL-COLUMN

The perimeter of the original square space was maintained and divided in half by a new type, the "wall-column," in this case a wall with a 400mm jog at its midpoint. The jog results in a gap which marks the geometric center of the square space. This slim passageway, with its narrow door for privacy, recalls the White Room column.

ALMOST-SYMMETRICAL PLANS

The addition of the wall-column creates two interlocking, L-shaped spaces of the same size. While the two rooms have identical floor plates, albeit in point reflection, and wood flooring that directs a parallel flow, there is much variation in the repetition.

At a glance, the two spaces appear centrally symmetric, but they are not. The guest room and kitchen both have doors to the hallway, but they are positioned differently; the kitchen has a unique second opening to the living-dining room. Both rooms have identical window-doors facing the garden and hugging the central wall-column, but the asymmetry of the two spaces frames the apertures differently. The guest room has no built-in furnishings, while the kitchen is differentiated by the addition of the requisite fixtures. The respective context and program of the two spaces create difference in the sameness.

GABLES

After carefully defining the two parallel spaces, the architects make a surprising, counterintuitive move: they rotate the gabled ceiling 90 degrees. In contradiction to the plan, the rotated ceiling *unites* the same two spaces the wall-column *divides*. Additionally, the ceiling's double gable, acting in collaboration with the jog in the wall-column, effectively transforms two rooms into four spaces: bedroom-wardrobe and kitchen-laundry.

This is architectural alchemy, pure and simple. To create such effect with nothing more than a wall, a door, two gabled ceilings and the relationships between them, is testament to the brilliance of Atelier Nishikata.

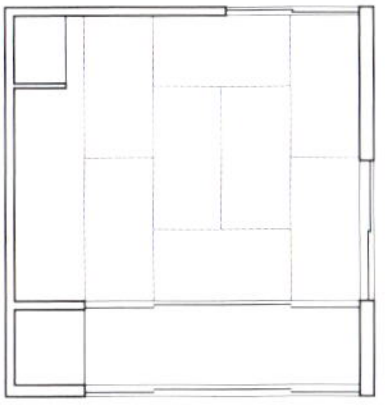
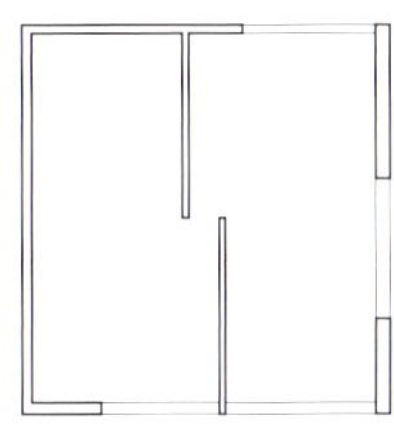
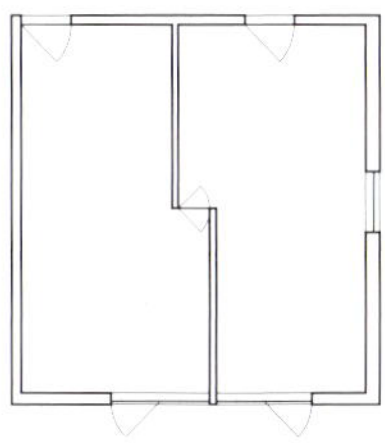
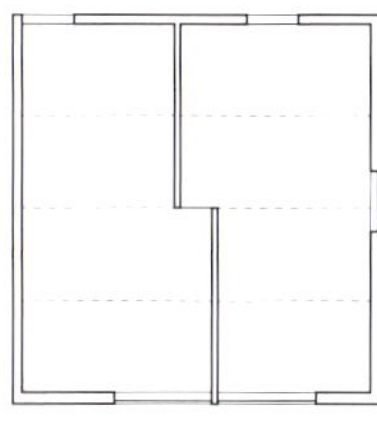

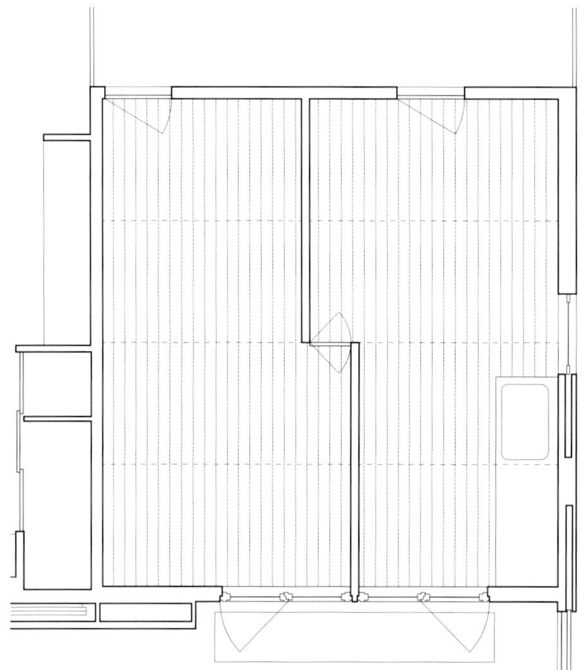

0
1
2
3m

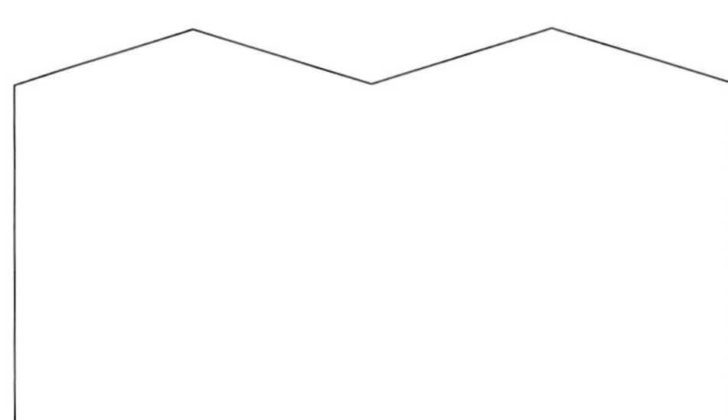

West

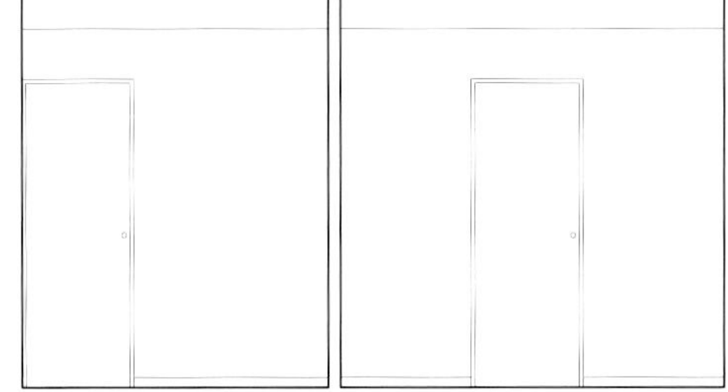

North

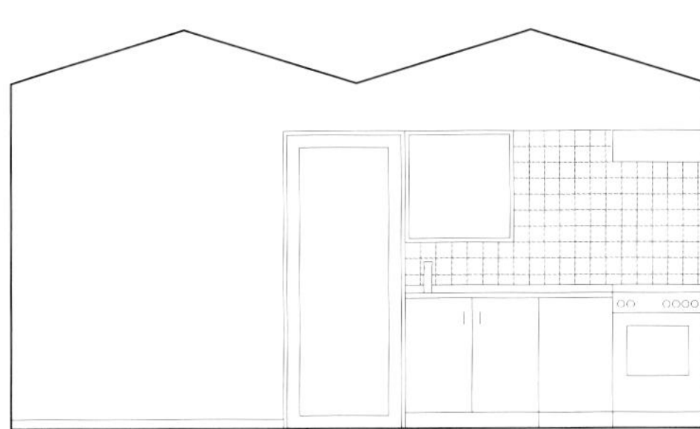

East

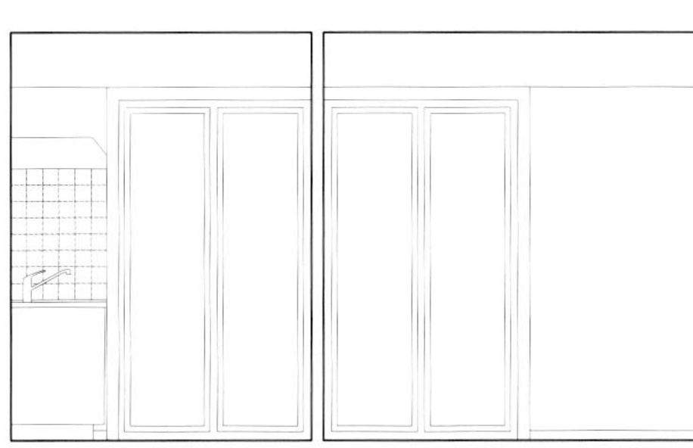

South

0 1 2 3m

III Black Room

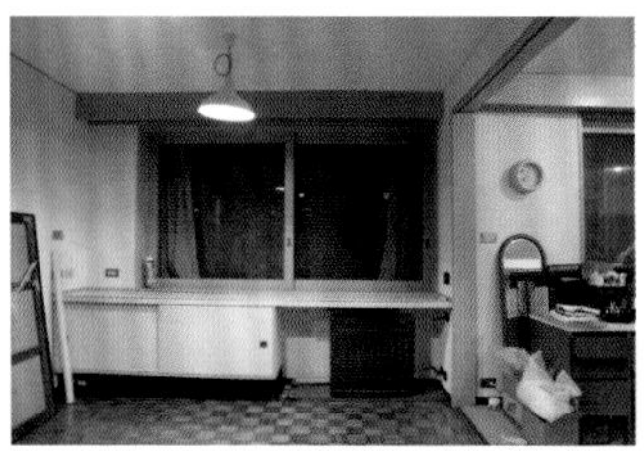

With a new kitchen provided in Moto-Washitsu and a living room large enough to host meals, the original dining room, kitchen, utility and boiler rooms at the southeast corner of the house could be walled off and reconfigured to form Room 101, the first of two rental units. Entered from the carport, the entry hall-dining room serves to separate the renovated kitchen and bathroom from the Black Room, the main living and working space.

As their names suggest, the Black Room and White Room are fraternal twins, with similarities and differences. The Black Room, like its sibling, is square, but slightly smaller. It too contains a large, free-standing column, but one quite unique in character. Its walls are also clad, albeit in a distinctly different material. The many relationships between the rooms provoke a sense of the "already seen."

COLUMN

While the columns in the White and Black Rooms serve a common purpose—to divide the space and create overlapping spatial transparencies that effectively enlarge the room perceptually—here the column marks the true center of the space, dividing the room into four equal parts. Additionally, both columns serve a structural function, but do so in distinct ways. In the White Room, the column's two supporting members frame the passage through a voided center. In the Black Room, the "box" column contains an x-shaped structural column within and offers no interior access. A knock on the 4mm-thin plywood cladding rings mysteriously hollow.

CLADDING

Every surface in the Black Room—walls and windows, floor and ceiling—is clad with plywood; even the centered column and the entry door are not spared. The plywood sheets were purchased in batches, matching the grain between pairs of panels as closely as possible to avoid a random pattern. As the standard piece of plywood in Japan measures 910mm x 1820mm, all the panels had to be trimmed.

As in the White Room, there are two conflicting rules guiding the cladding design. In the Black Room, the first specifies that all the plywood panels (with the exception of those cladding the column) be of equal width: 868mm. Twelve fixed panels on each elevation, arranged in two rows of six, are cut to a length of 1150mm. The floor panels, eighteen of them in three rows of six, have a length of 1736mm and are oriented east-west. The ceiling mirrors the floor but rotates 90

degrees establishing a relationship with the twisted ceiling in Moto-Washitu. With the length of the floor and ceiling panels double the width of all the panels, their seams align with the vertical seams on the walls.

The second rule specifies plywood panels of different sizes to shutter the existing apertures. Two large windows facing the garden to the south are covered respectively by four plywood shutters of one size, and two of another. A small third window on the opposite wall facing the main entry courtyard is shuttered with two panels of yet another dimension. In each case, piano hinges allow the folding shutters to lay flat against the wall when opened.

Again here, as in the White Room, the misalignment between the rules guiding the fixed plywood cladding and the operable shuttering systems creates a tension between the two. But this room is quieter than its twin, with far less architectural crosstalk. Given its program as a live-work space for two inhabitants, no doubt the relative silence is most welcome.

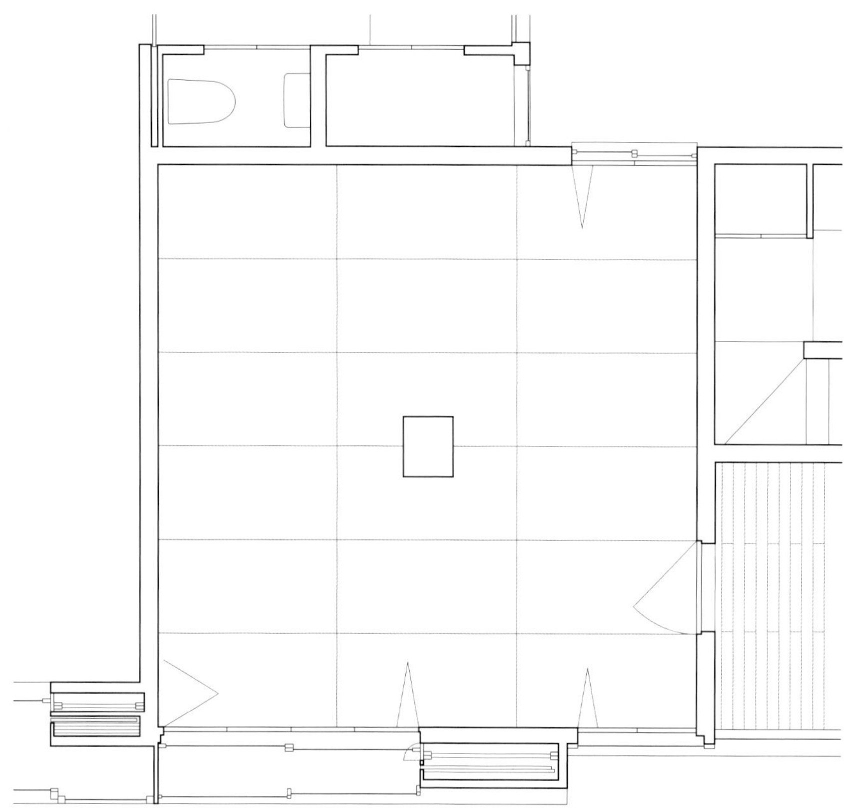

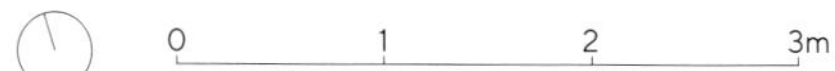
0
1
2
3m

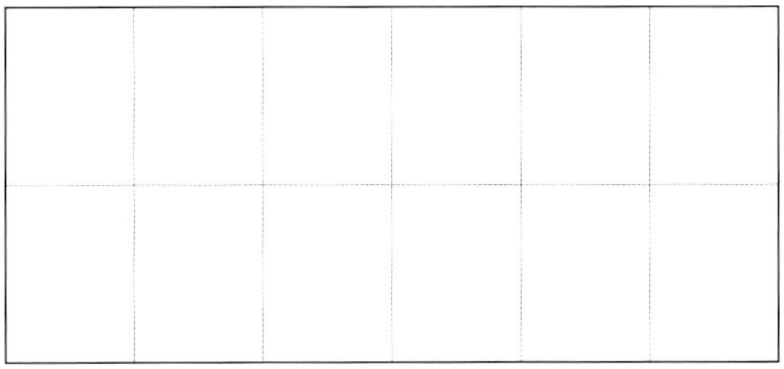

West

North

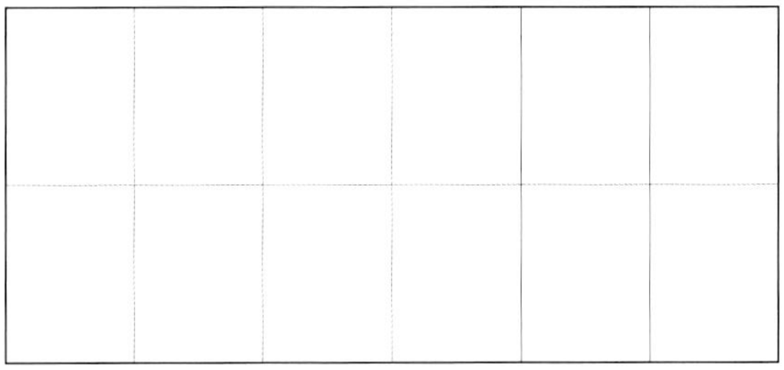

East

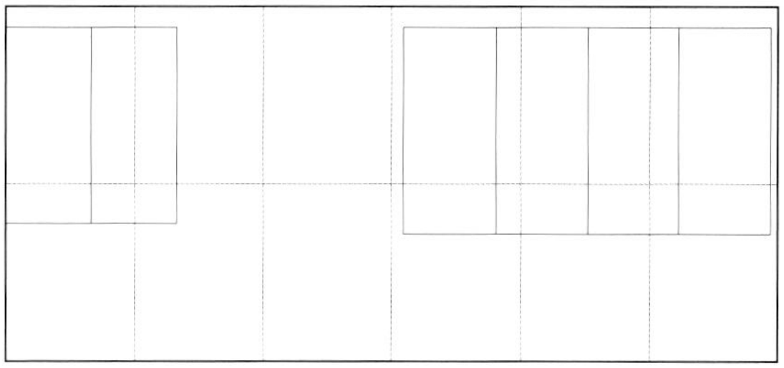

South

0 1 2 3m

IV Diamond Room

The Diamond Room is embedded within the only second-story space in the house. Originally accessed from the interior, the conversion of the space to an autonomous rental apartment, Room 201, required a reconfiguration of the ground-floor entry sequence. The new front door is accessed from the street, through a dedicated gate and a small, private courtyard. After entering a small vestibule, a winding stair leads to the living spaces on the upper level.

To convert the space into a fully functioning apartment for two, the renovation involved the addition of a quiet study separated from the main living space, a full bathroom with tub and a walk-in closet. A new kitchen would have a dedicated nook within the open studio space.

LOBBY + EIGHT DOORS

At the top of the stairs, an enlarged landing-study, separated from the main living space by the Diamond Room, provides a degree of privacy in the small, shared apartment. Here one is confronted with two narrow doors. We have seen these doors before, sometimes as singles, sometimes as doubles. They are the same doors we passed through to enter and depart the White Room, the same doors that turned a column into a closet, then a window, then a passageway. It is the same door that permitted or denied access through the wall-column in Moto-Washitsu. Here those same doors are re-contextualized and framed uniquely by two walls set at 45 degrees acting as a human funnel.

Upon opening the doors, one enters the Diamond Room, the heart of the renovated apartment. Rotated 45 degrees to the house plan, the Diamond Room is a minuscule space just one meter square. This tiny room is defined by a unique parquet floor (reminiscent of Loos's alcove in the Villa Müller) and four elevations composed entirely of identical pairs of double doors. Standing inside the room with all the doors closed, one might imagine being inside the inaccessible interior of the Black Room column.

As in TV game shows where behind each door a different prize awaits the contestant, each pair of doors in the Diamond Room conceals a different program. Behind Doors #1, the landing-study; Doors #2, the bathroom; Doors #4, the walk-in closet; Doors #3 reveal the jackpot: the kitchen and main living space.

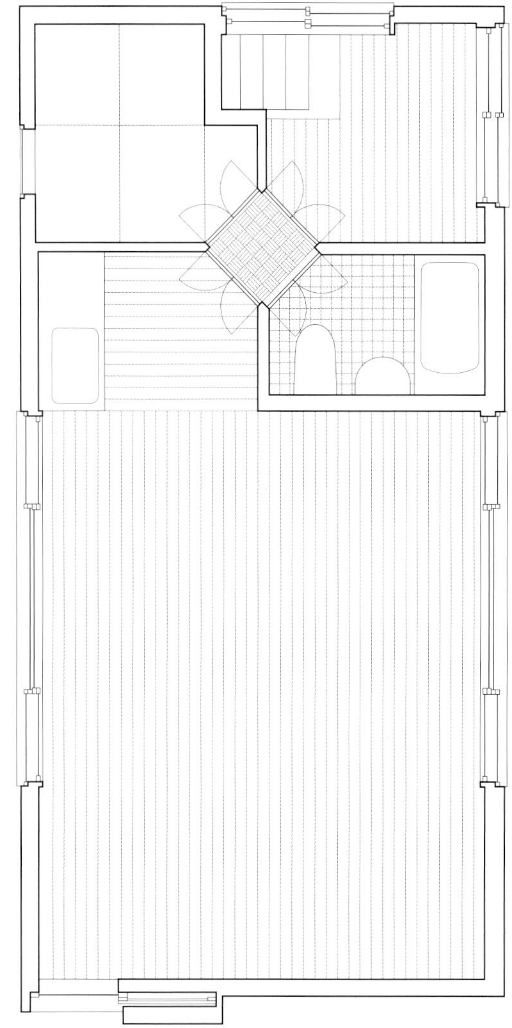

0
1
2
3m

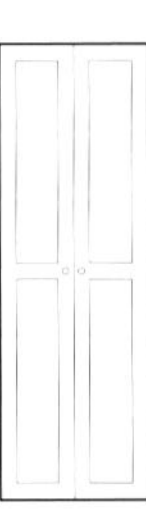

Northwest

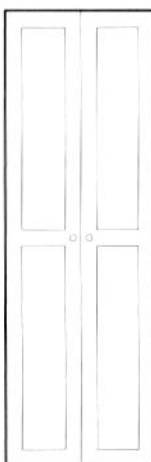

Northeast

Southwest

Southeast

0 1 2 3m

MARY GOES ROUND

Mary Goes Round is the renovation of a classic, four-room apartment in a modest six-story building in Kawasaki near Tokyo. The four quadrants originally housed the entry-kitchen, a living room, a traditional tatami room used for sleeping and a bathroom. The aim was to refresh the rental unit with a thorough "whitewashing" and to perceptually expand its size by increasing its spatial complexity.

COLUMN

Repeating a strategy deployed in the White and Black Rooms, Atelier Nishikata introduced a central column. This time, however, the column is not in the center of a room, but rather in the center of the apartment. By occupying the intersection of the four rooms, the small post reserves for itself the only possible 360-degree view. In this project, the column is not inhabited, it is personified.

The column defines a new, small space: the *futokoro*. The literal translation of *futokoro* is inside pocket, but other meanings include: money; a space surrounded by outstretched arms and the chest; a deep rear place surrounded by mountains; a safe place separated from the outside world; inside; one's mind. The introduction of a fifth space in a four-square apartment has significant spatial implications.

FLOORING

With the removal of the tatami mats, the addition of new wood flooring in the traditional room unifies the three main living spaces. Light inlaid wood strips radiating from the column delineate the boundaries of the primary spaces and provide tracks for new sliding doors.

WALLS

Only two walls required significant reconfiguration. The new wall between the kitchen and living space was halved along its length, one half solidified to shield the kitchen appliances, and the other half nearest the column, left open. The new wall between the living room and the bedroom, after accounting for a large corner column, was also divided in two: one half solid (with a pocket), one half open. These alterations leave the central column free, and well, Mary Goes Round.

DOORS

Three new doors—a glass slider with a four-square frame referencing the floor plan and the exterior windows, an opaque pocket door, and a glazed swing door—interact with the column to create a wealth of new spatial configurations. When all the doors are closed, the column becomes a doorframe and the *futokoro* transforms the four-room classic into a five-room apartment.

Mary Goes Round is an exemplary case of the literal and phenomenal transparencies described in Colin Rowe's and Robert Slutsky's influential essay.[1] As the three doors open and close in the dance of daily life, the number of spaces and their boundaries are in constant flux.

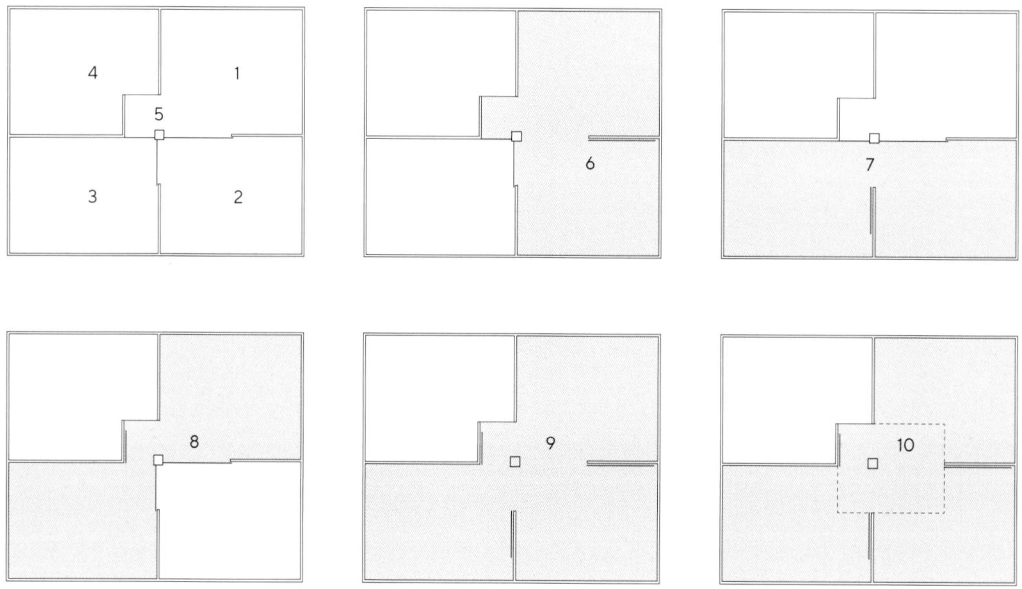

1. Colin Rowe and Robert Slutzky, "Transparency: Literal and Phenomenal," *Perspecta* 8 (1963): 45–54.

BEFORE

1. Kitchen-dining
2. Living Room
3. Tatami Room
4. Bathroom

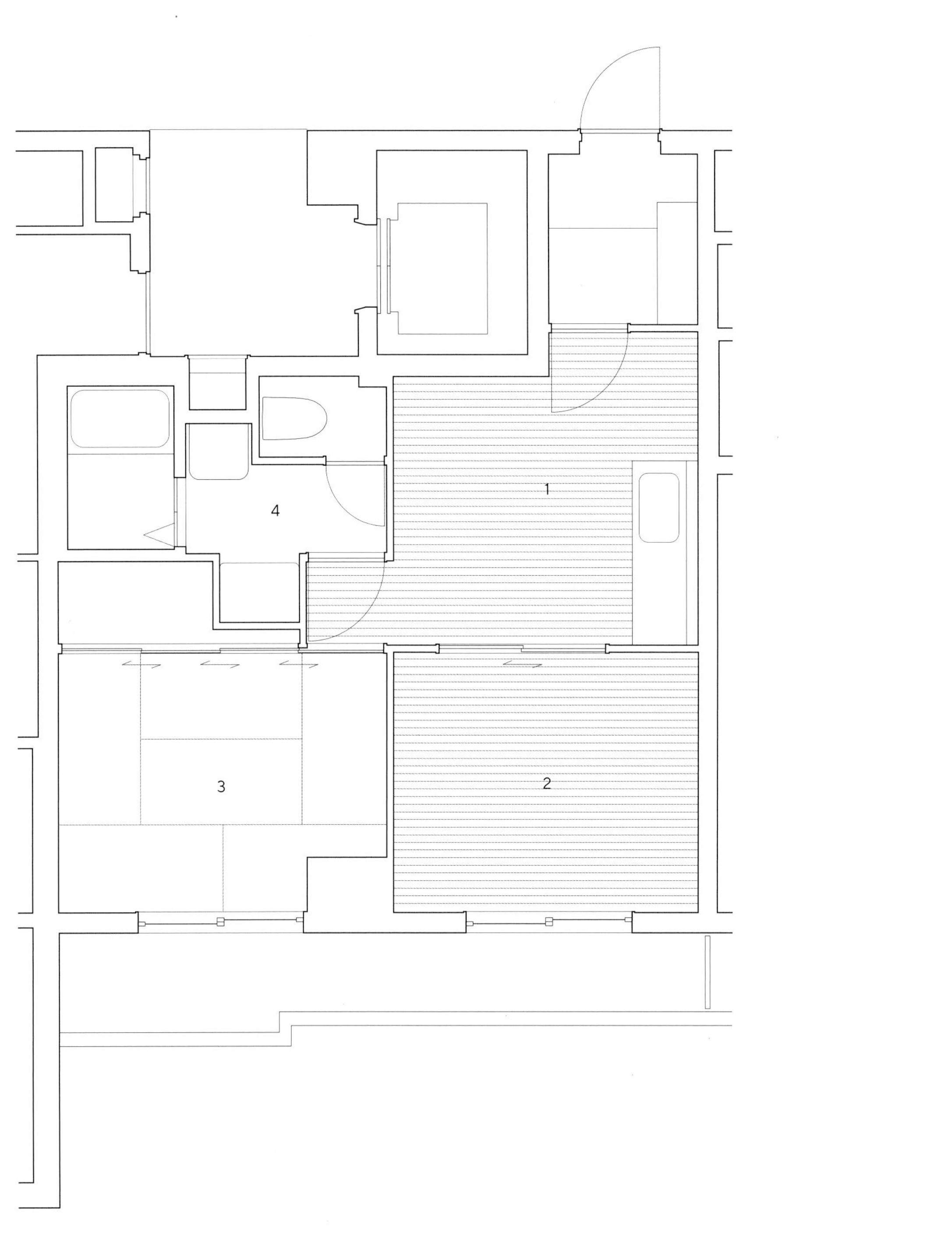

AFTER

1. Kitchen-dining
2. Room One
3. Room Two
4. Bathroom
5. Futokoro

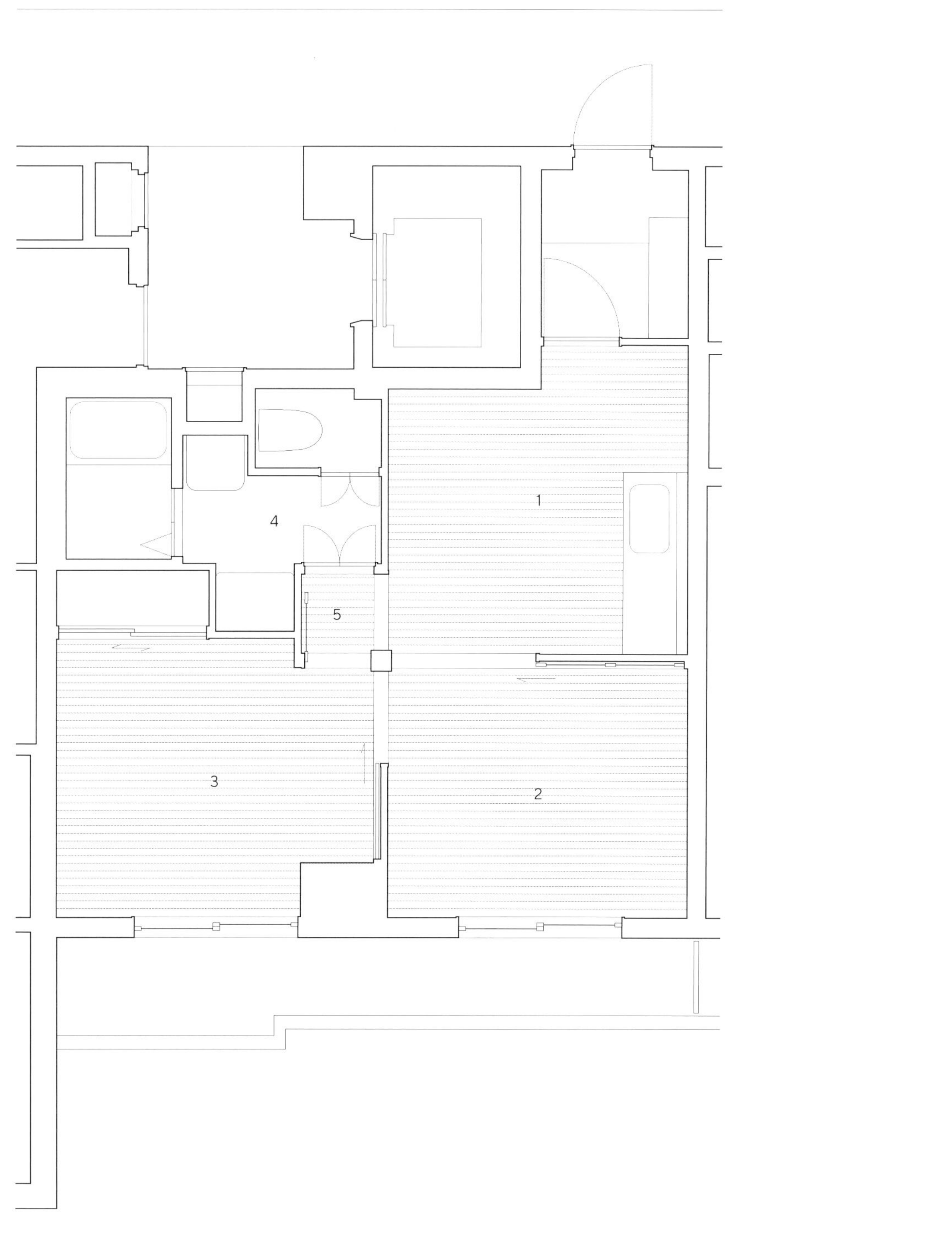

FRAME

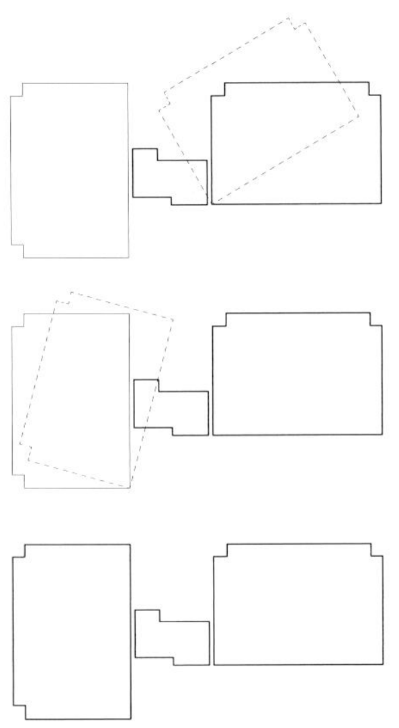

COPYPAY (copy and paste)

Frame was commissioned by a friend following the passing of his parents. The task was to connect the family's two penthouse apartments to create a commodious live-work space for the photographer, his wife and two sons. The two apartments would be joined while preserving the ability to separate them again in the future.

The architects began this project by establishing similitude between the two dissimilar apartments, a familiar strategy used in earlier projects. In each of the Four Episodes, for example, all new spaces were created equally square and each was outfitted with a box- or wall-column. In Mary Goes Round, the three primary living spaces were materially homogenized and reconfigured around a shared, central column. And as we will soon see in House in Awaji, the four levels start with identical floor plans.

PLAN

In this project, the architects first excavated a large rectangle, Frame I, from the plan of the western unit. Within the larger project called Frame, Frame I circumscribed the existing kitchen, living and dining rooms, one bedroom and the sunken entry hall. Only the master bedroom, study and bathroom fell outside this first frame. A second rectangle, Frame II, a near-exact replica of Frame I, was rotated 90 degrees and superimposed on the plan of the eastern apartment, the former home of the client's parents.

This process of copying an original on a remote site recalls the Japanese tradition of *utsushi* in which a revered work of art or architecture is appropriated from a distance.[1] As *utsushi* is a means for respectfully connecting the past with the present and future, the tradition has particular resonance in this story of three generations.

ANTEROOM

Frames I and II are separated by an anteroom-library adjacent to the children's bedroom. By skewing the checkerboard flooring to align with true north, the architects disrupt the spatial alignment between Frames I and II, expanding the perceived distance between the two spaces. The anteroom serves as a palette cleanser between Frames I and II.

1. For more on Atelier Nishikata and *utsushi,* see Reiko Nishio and Hirohito Ono, "Frame - 'Utsushi:' Uraku, Korin, and Irises," *Atelier Nishikata,* https://atelier-nishikata.info/writing/textpage/frame_en.

WALLPAPER

Both Frames are reinforced by a band of wallpaper encircling the space, serving a similar function as the three ledges in the White Room. But as always in the architecture of Atelier Nishikata, sameness must be complimented by difference; while the wallpaper bands ringing the two frames are both designed by William Morris, each boasts a different color and pattern. And as in the White Room, the bands that help define the space must be interrupted, in this case not by vertical cladding joints, but by door and window frames.

DOOR AND WINDOW FRAMES

A comparison of the interior elevations of Frame I and II is astounding: the location of the large columns and all the framed openings, both doorways and windows, are identically positioned and sized. There are new large frames with double sliding doors, and small frames with single sliders; there are window frames and frames for conventional doors. There are frames that frame frames. While creating this similitude required some renovation, this achievement is nonetheless remarkable given the dissimilarity of the two original units.

While the interior elevations are identical between the two Frames, behind the many twinned apertures, differences abound. Any two identical apertures frame different programs, different views, different solar orientations, different wallpaper patterns. Opening the doors and exposing the differences recalls the Diamond Room experience.

The deployment of frames, with their sameness and difference, was inspired by Yasujirō Ozu's *Tokyo Story*. In the film, as elderly parents' visit their grown children in different Japanese cities, each new domestic scene repeats a similar framing. The configuration of architectural frames, and the positioning of the props and actors, repeats itself over and over as the households change. This repetition variation, a technique employed regularly by Ozu in his films, and employed in Frame by Atelier Nishikata, evokes a false sense of familiarity that is at the heart of the déjà vu experience. While one cannot actually experience again what one has yet to experience for the first time, when moving between frames we seem to do exactly that.

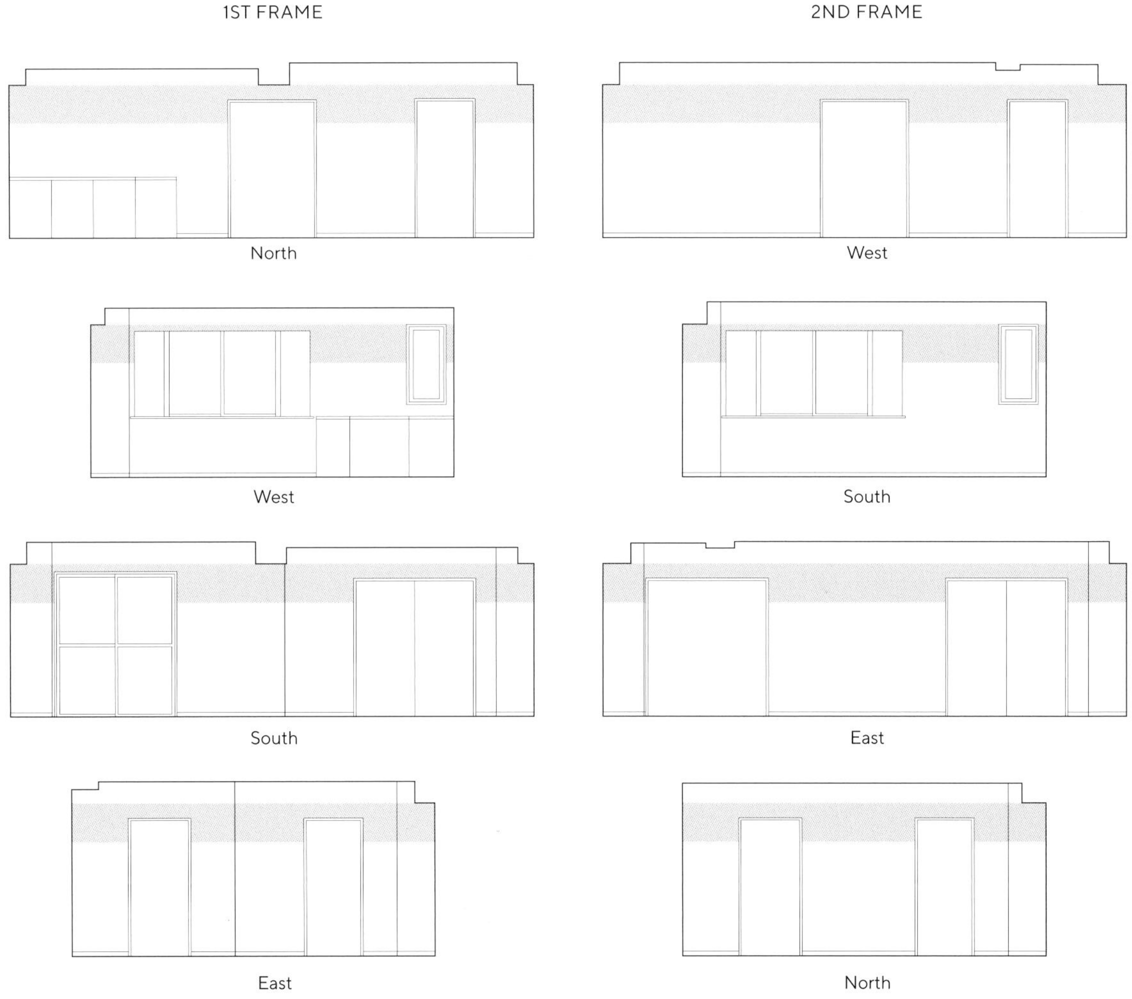

Full-scale mock-up of Frame II

Tokyo Story
Yasujirō Ozu

BEFORE

602
1. Entry Hall
2. Kitchen, Living, and Dining Room
3. Bedroom
4. Study
5. Master Bedroom

601
6. Entry Hall
7. Living and Dining Room
8. Kitchen
9. Tatami Room
10. Bedroom

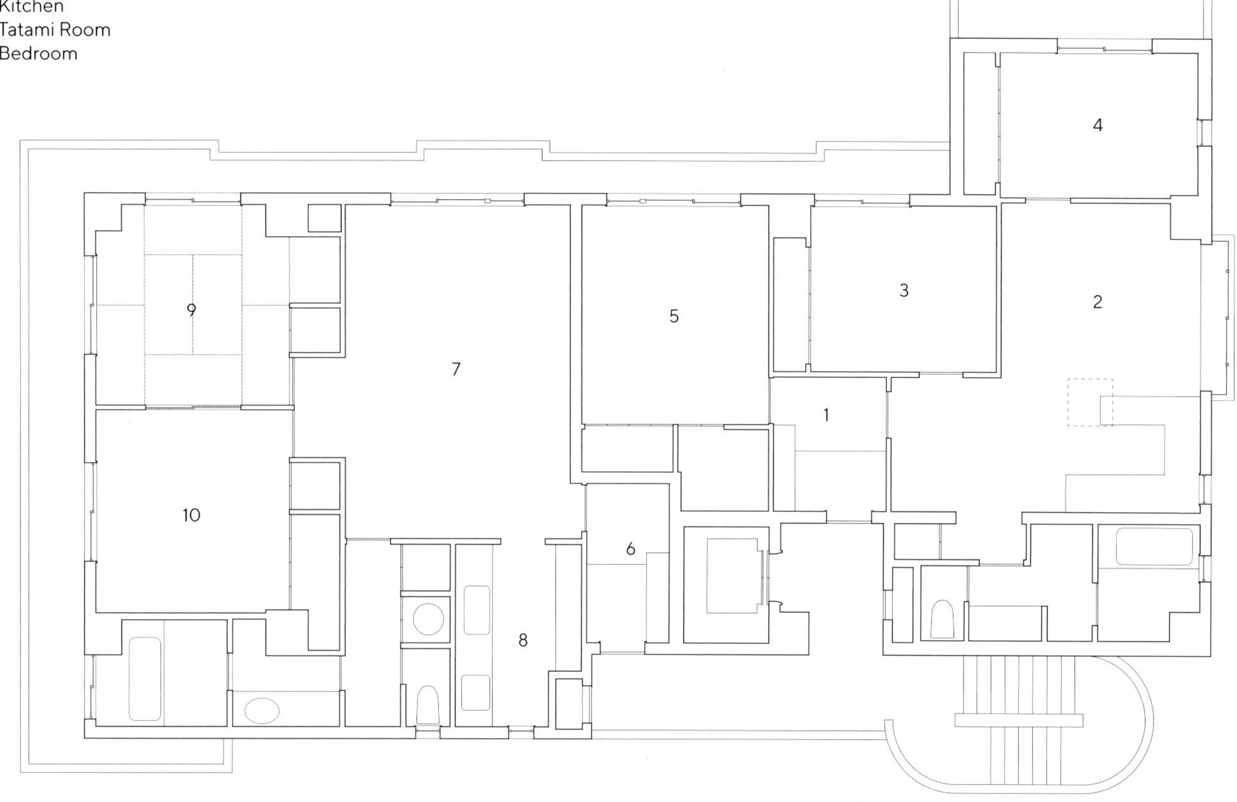

AFTER

1. Frame I: Gallery, Studio
2. Frame II: Kitchen, Living, and Dining Room
3. Anteroom Library
4. Children's Bedroom
5. Master Bedroom
6. Study
7. Guest Room

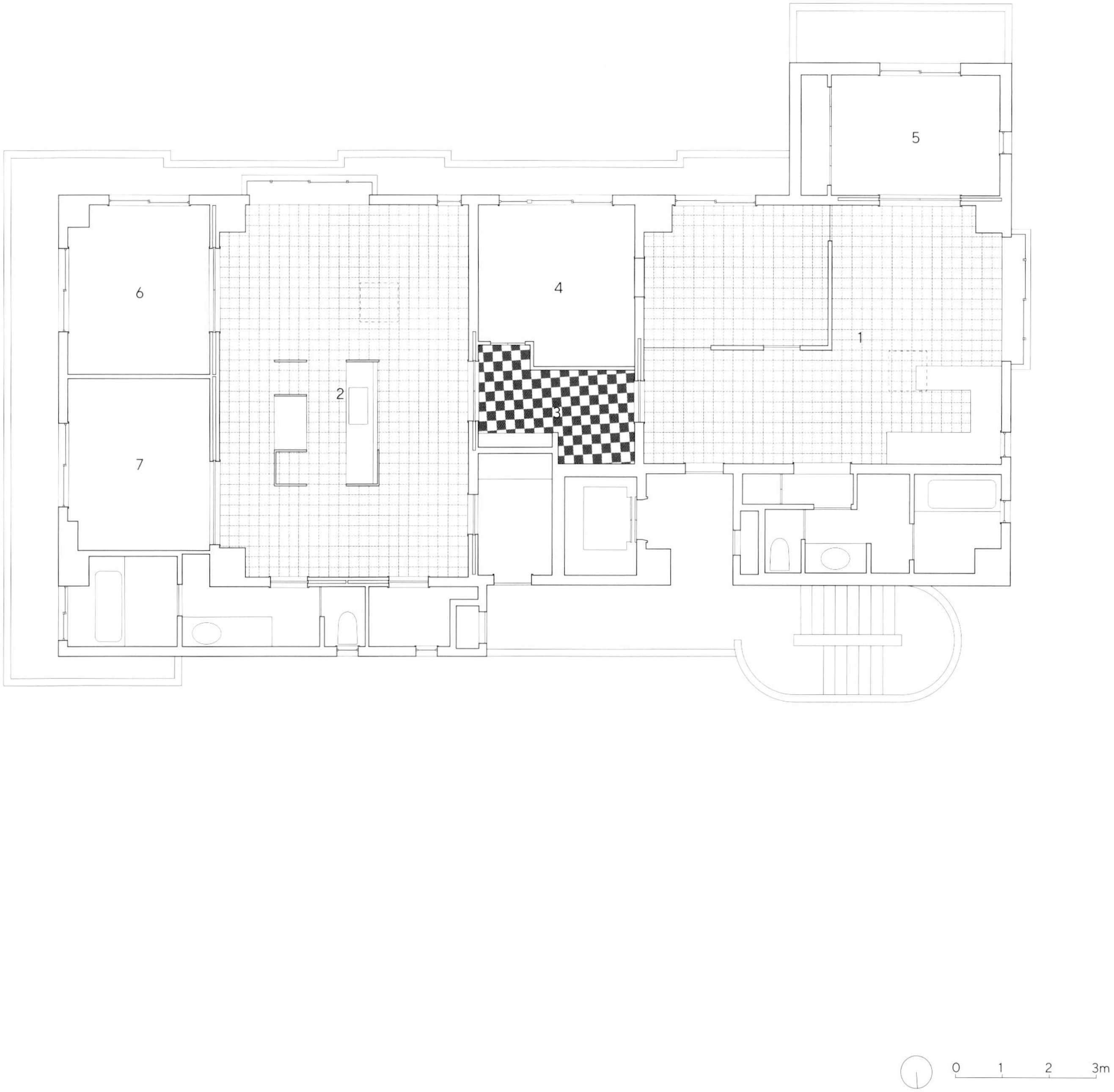

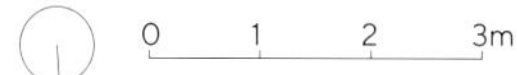

HOUSE IN AWAJI

Atelier Nishikata's first commission was the design of a residence for a bachelor on the site of an old bicycle repair shop in Chiyoda, Tokyo. The new house would be sandwiched between a seven-story office building to the east and a three-story house to the west, with gaps between them of only 55cm and 30cm respectively. To the south, a small court offered minimal access to light; to the north, Awaji Park provided an expanse view.

PLAN + SECTION

While the narrow plot, just 3.5m x 8.5m, might suggest maximizing the glazing to the north and keeping the plan as open as possible, Atelier Nishikata took a very different approach. In their words: "If you see everything at once, the sense of space cannot expand beyond the actual dimensions." The architects divided each of the four floors into two rooms—one rectangular, one square—separated by an enclosed, single-run staircase. The eight living spaces have distinct floor levels determined by the varying stair configurations in the four stacked stairwells. Both the consistent floor plans and the varying sections are determined by the same 1:√2 proportional system.

PUBLIC-PRIVATE PROGRAMS

In a consequential decision, the architects designated four of the living spaces as "public" (guests are welcome) and four as "private" (off-limits to guests). The public rooms and the private rooms are equally likely to be located at the front of the house in the larger spaces or in the smaller spaces facing the light court. Their staggered distribution thwarts any easy front-back, rectangular-square, or level-by-level reading of the house.

8 bedroom (private - rectangular - front)
7 sunroom/bathroom (public - square - rear)
6 living room (public - rectangular - front)
5 kitchen (private - square - rear)
4 entry/music room (public - rectangular - front)
3 study (private - square - rear)
2 storage (private - rectangular - front)
1 guest room (public - square - rear)

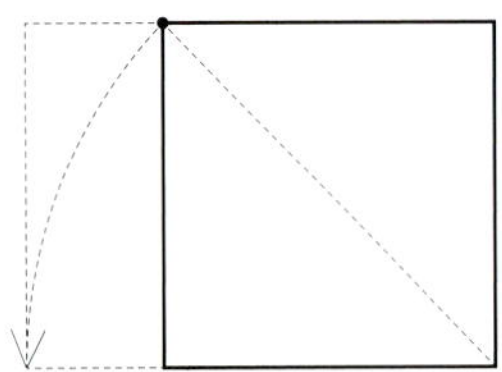

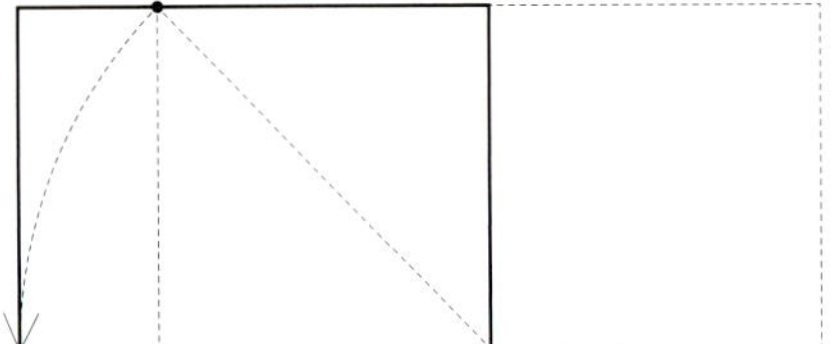

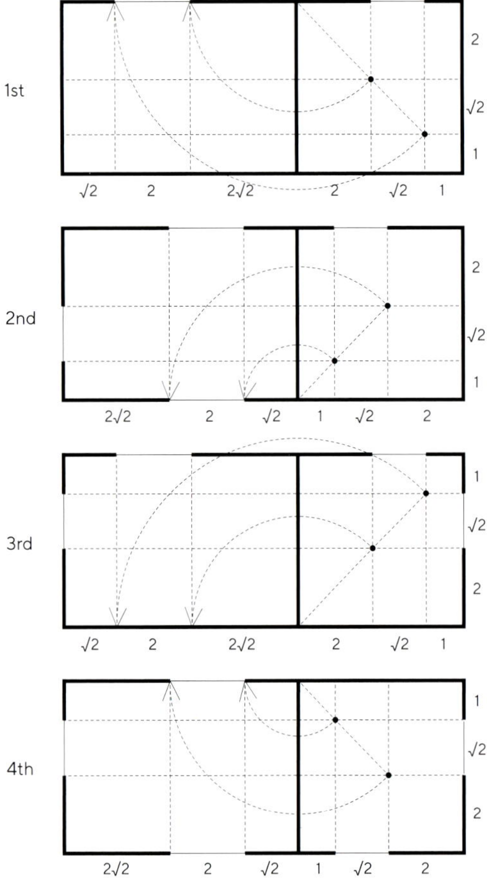
1st
2
√2
1
√2 2 2√2 2 √2 1
2nd
2
√2
1
2√2 2 √2 1 √2 2
3rd
1
√2
2
√2 2 2√2 2 √2 1
4th
1
√2
2
2√2 2 √2 1 √2 2

U-shape, S-shape mirrored

STAIRS

The single-run, two-step winder stair appears in three different forms in the four stacked stairwells: S-shape mirrored (twice), U-shape (once) and S-shape (once.) The split in the landings at the top and bottom of each run varies, biasing a path that connects the designated public spaces.

The complex circulation starts at the public guest room on the lowest of the eight levels. From there, the first of two "S-shape mirrored" stairs breezes past the storage room and, one flight up, the study (both private rooms) to arrive at the public entry-music room. This is the first of the four public spaces that serve as switchbacks. From this main street-level entry, a "U-shape" stair leads past the private kitchen to the living room overhead. This public room then serves as the second switchback. The only "S-shaped stair" then leads from the living room in the front of the house, to the sunroom/bathroom, up one flight at the rear of the house. This space, somewhat surprisingly designated as public, then serves as the final switchback. One circulates through the sunroom, past an enclosed water closet and separate bathing area, to reach the final stair. This second "S-shape mirrored" stair passes by the private bedroom and offers access to the roof.

The interior walls of the four stacked stairwells are clad with steel panels, factory-painted with grey rustproof paint. The default, industrial finish on the panels, more typically smoothed over with a coat of interior paint, was left intentionally rough to acknowledge the "readymade" status of the panels.

Visitors en route to the public spaces naturally bypass the private rooms with their closed, hinged doors painted to match the stairwell panels. Sliding doors into the public rooms are generally left open. Viewed from the interior of the public living spaces, the opened doors blend with the plywood paneling while the same doors in their closed position reveal steel panels and structural pillars.

CEILING VAULTS

One might expect a vault to be reserved for the most important space, or maybe even two, but in House in Awaji there is no discrimination between spaces. No matter their program, whether a storage room or living room, all spaces are treated as equals. Nishio and Ono explain: "We thought that flat ceilings make it hard for the rooms to create spatial relationships with each other, because they cannot enhance the independence and character of each room. If all the ceilings were flat, that would just boost the locational gap between the rectangular rooms facing the park and the square rooms at the rear of the site. So we first wanted to set up the eight rooms in a spatially equal state. Next, we considered adding operations such as the orientation of the stairs and the direction of the barrel vaults to create a hierarchy between public and private rooms."

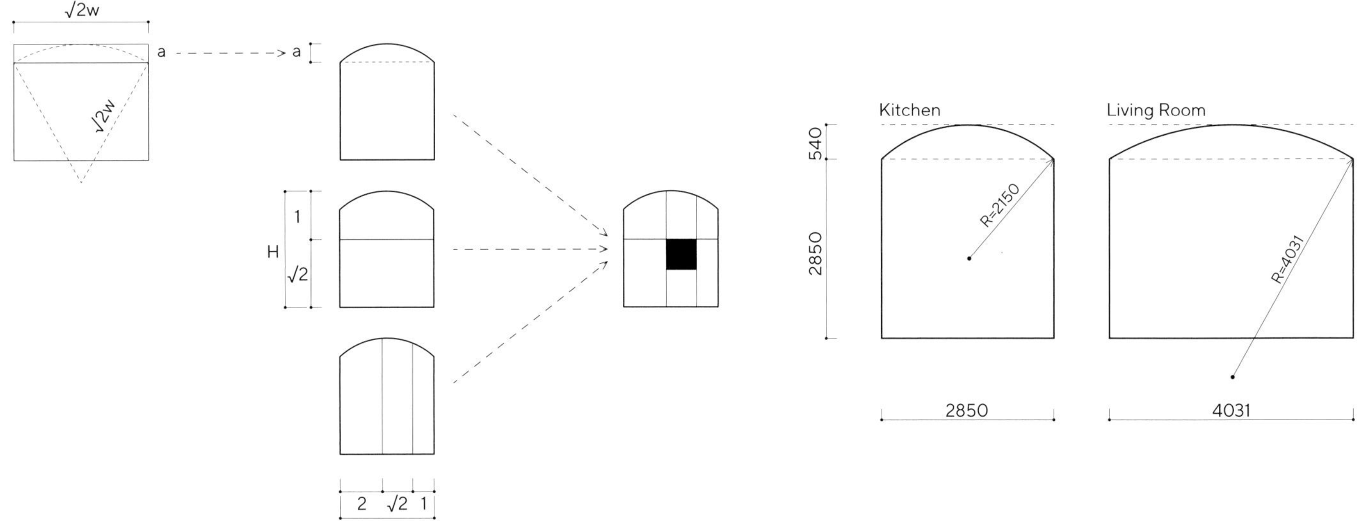

The ceilings are *almost* barrel vaults, but not, as they serve no structural purpose and, in the case of the square rooms, their width and length are equal. All the vaults in the house have one of two radii—2150mm or 4031mm—a system inspired by Le Cobusier's Maison Jaoul. The radius 4031 is equal to the length of the rectangular rooms. Drawing a circular arc with the radius 4031 determines the chord height, which is then applied to the smaller vault as well. The radius of 2150 is thus determined.

The vaults in the private rooms spring from the east and west walls, while the vaults in the public rooms turn 90 degrees and launch from walls on the north and south. This counterintuitive orientation of the vaults in the entry and living room intentionally counteracts any natural bias towards the park view by "turning attention to the internal spatial structure." There is one exception to the rule guiding the orientation of the vaults: the vault in the private kitchen deviates to align with the vault in public living room, creating a lateral "M" connection between the two programmatically related spaces.

CANTED WALLS

The four public rooms are further distinguished by a canted wall on alternating elevations. In the guest room (level 1 - rear) and living room (level 6 - front), the east wall is canted; in the entry-room (level 4 - front) and sunroom (level 7 - rear), the west wall. The sloping walls allow light to penetrate the interior through the narrow gap that reveals the non-structural nature of the vaults. The dramatic, almost sacred effect of the light raking over the walls is stunning, and surprising, considering only 55cm and 30cm separate the house from its neighbors.

CLADDING

Every space in the house is lined with highly textured Lauan plywood. The two consistent widths of the panels, 646mm and 913mm, are based on the same 1:√2 proportions used to generate the plans. As in the Black Room, the only other Atelier Nishikata space to be completely cloaked in plywood, the vertical joints in the wall cladding tie the walls and ceilings together. It is worth noting, however, that these continuous joints are never aligned with the centre of the space.

A single, horizontal recess encircles each room, its height determined by dividing the height of the room (from floor to the top of the vaulted ceiling) by 1:√2. Inspired by the Shaker tradition, the recess provides opportunities for hanging pictures and mirrors, hats and coats, portable shelves for books and kitchen goods. Even the windows in this house appear to "hang" from this same horizontal line.

APERTURES

The windows fall into place, aligned with the cladding system, both horizontally and vertically. The proportions of the windows, 1:1 or 1:√2, follow the proportions of the plan and the cladding. There are just four different windows, in four different sizes: two square and two rectangular. Depending on their context, the rules allow for the rectangular windows to be oriented either vertically or horizontally.

The windows in the three rectangular rooms above grade—entry-music room, living room, master bedroom—are equipped with sliding wood panels to block the light and views as desired. The exterior of the panels facing the park are painted black in a nod to René Magritte's *Empire of Light*. (Only later did the architects realize the parallels with Marcel Duchamp's *Fresh Widow*.) The readymade windows and door on the street facade come with standard four-sided aluminum frames, but the manufacturer agreed to "assist" the windows by fabricating custom three-sided frames. The windows and the door share a common opening mechanism, but while the windows slide open to the right, the door slides open to the left in a playful counterpoint. This composition is set into a facade clad with sheets of asphalt roofing.

To position the windows on the east and west facades, the architects studied drawings of the neighbors' side elevations to avoid embarrassing alignments. Once those blackout zones were established, picture windows positioned on the side walls framed surprisingly compelling views of pipes and vent caps, successfully offering a counterpoint to the distant park vista.

Having established rules for the location and size of the windows, rules meant to establish a degree of sameness between the rooms, the architects introduced difference. In identical rooms—for example, the two private, rectangular rooms for storage and the master bedroom—the position of the window was flipped in one space to introduce variation within the repetition.

Unlike the windows, the height and width of the doors have an independent logic that *almost* aligns with the harmonious cladding and window system, but doesn't. While all the door heads have the same height, the window heads vary. Therefore, in some rooms the door head is higher than the top of the window, in others it is lower.

Nishio and Ono are comfortable playing devil's advocate, adopting counterintuitive strategies at every turn. The architects challenge normative assumptions about views and vaults and just about everything else. They add layer after layer of rules, aligning some, misaligning others, embracing necessary deviants. Most importantly, they always, always insist on difference in sameness.

While rules abound for the different components—vaults and cladding, stairs, windows and doors—what is of greatest importance is the relationships established between components. The picture window is in dialogue with the skylight above the canted wall; the sliding door in the entry-music room is in dialogue with the cladding and the apertures. The public guest room speaks to the public sunroom three levels above, while the kitchen speaks with the living room just across the stair. The poetic images engendered by these lively, crisscrossing exchanges exceed the limits of the small plywood and steel box giving space to the imagination.

Window position study

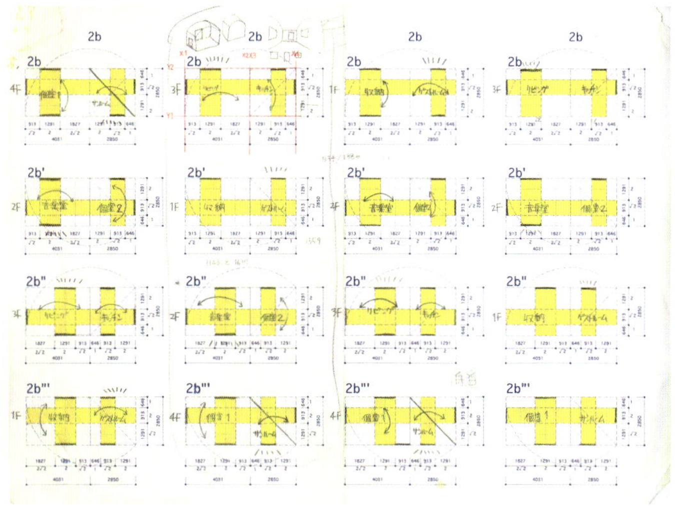

kamio
memorial
hospital
30

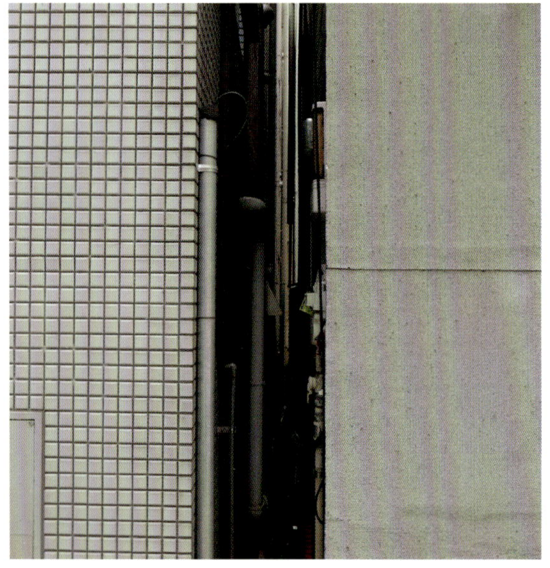

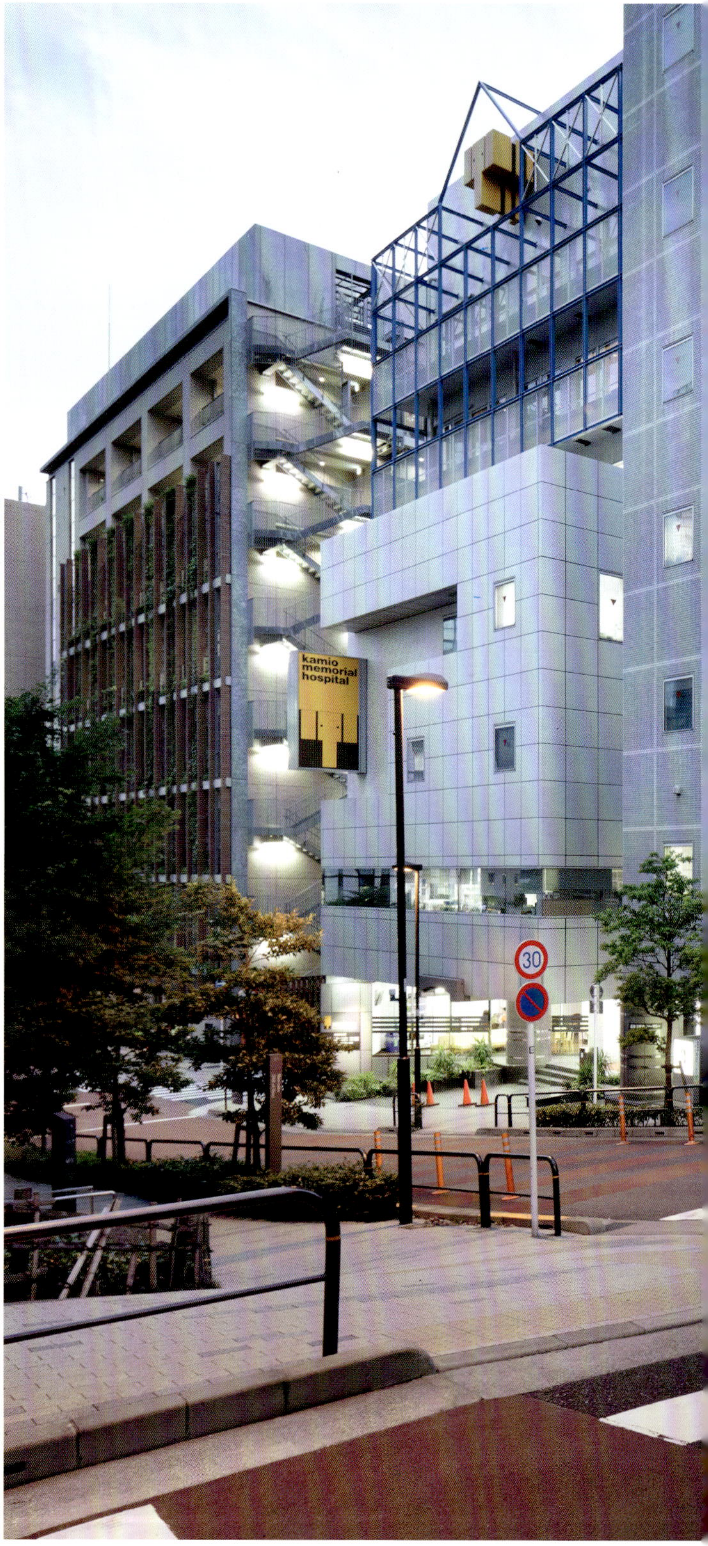

30

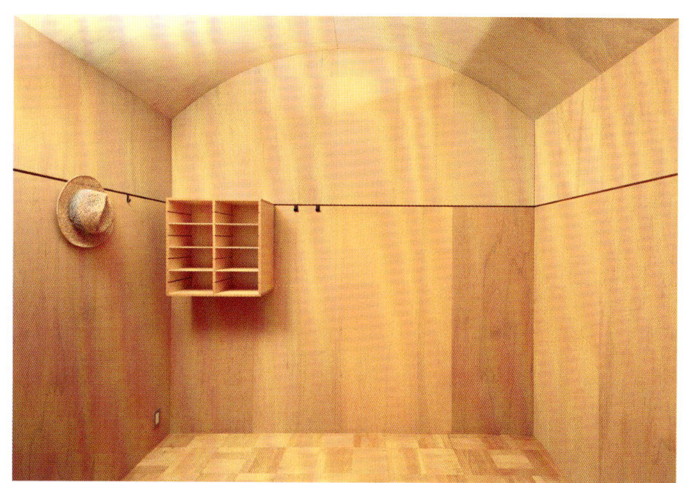

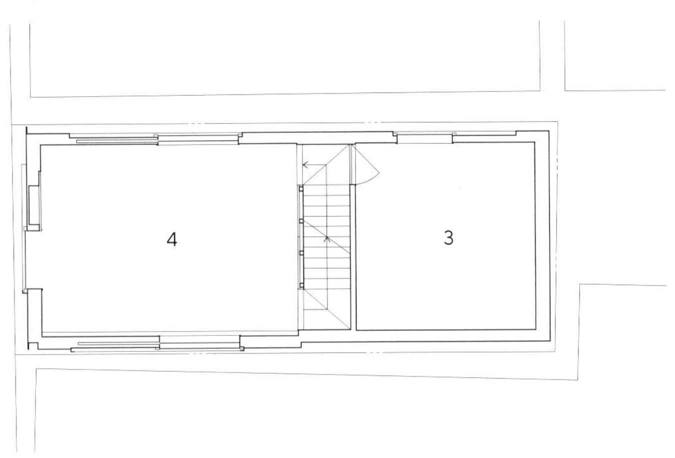

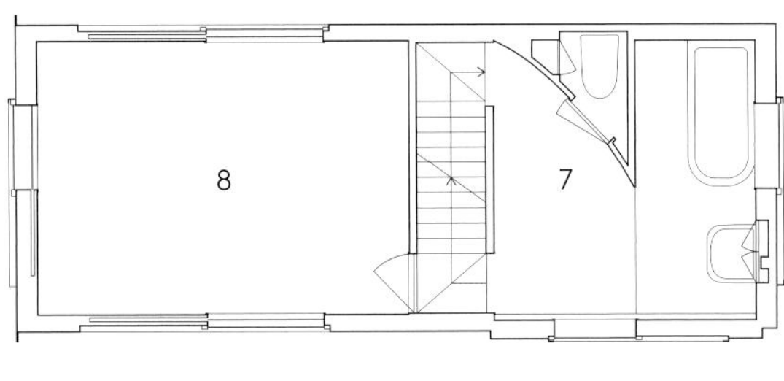

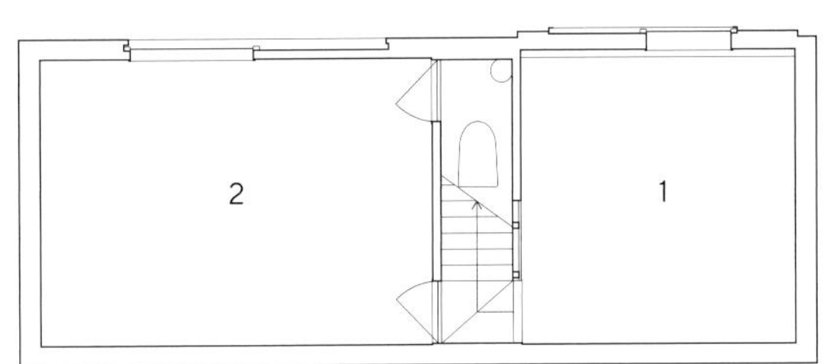

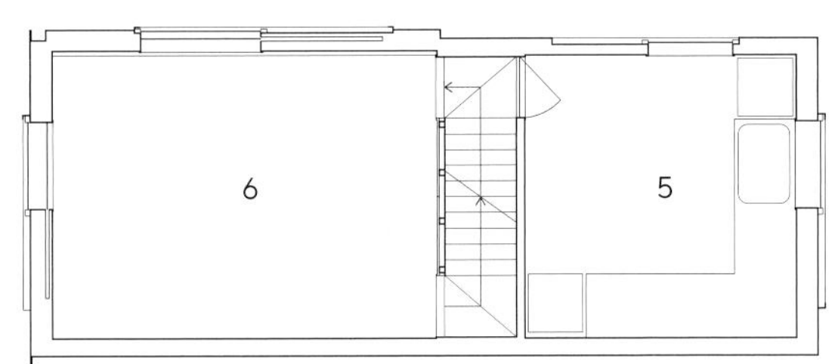

Basement Floor
1. Guest room
2. Storage

First Floor
3. Study
4. Entrance and music room

Second Floor
5. Kitchen
6. Living room

Third Floor
7. Sunroom
8. Master bedroom

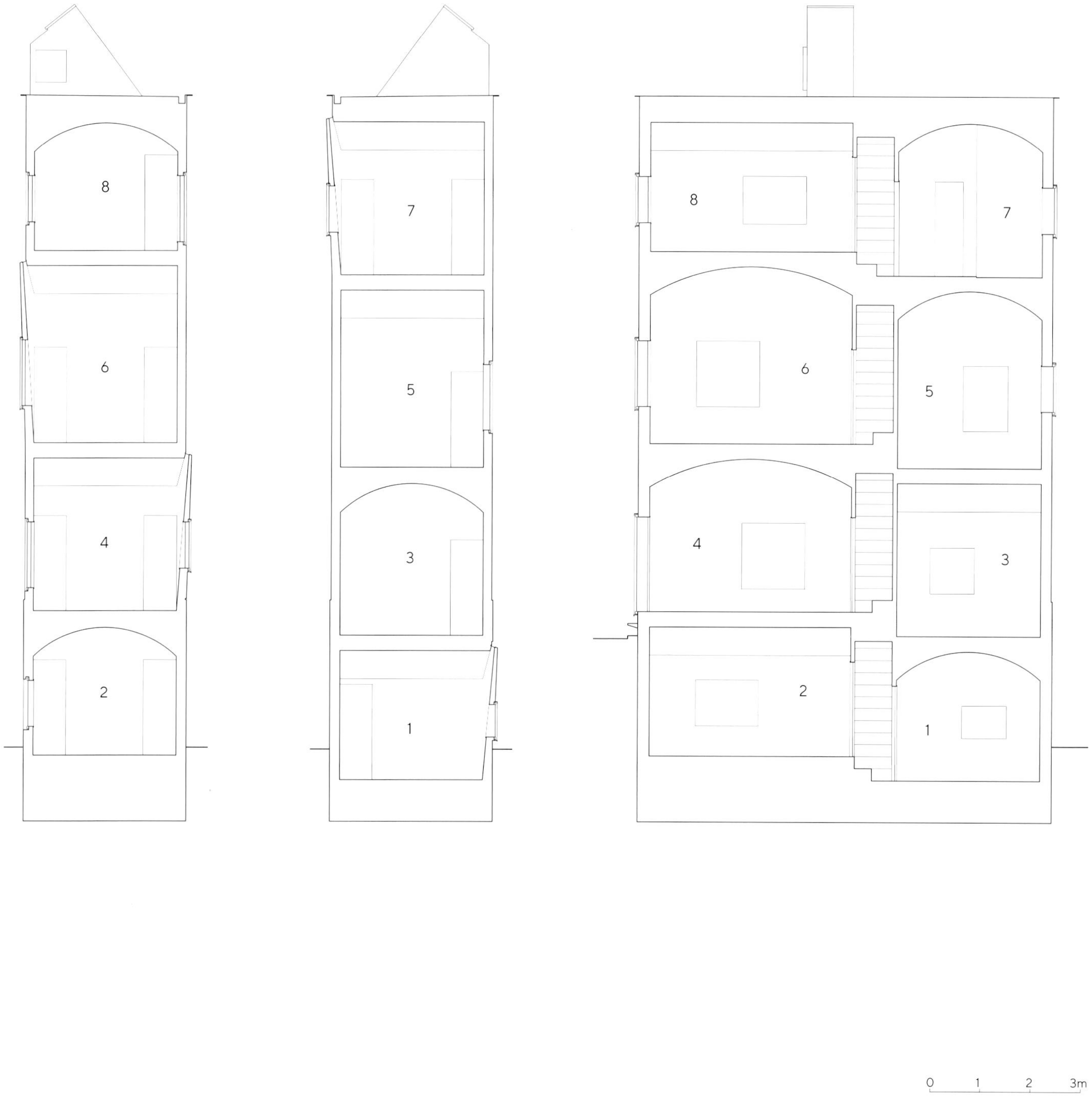

0 1 2 3m

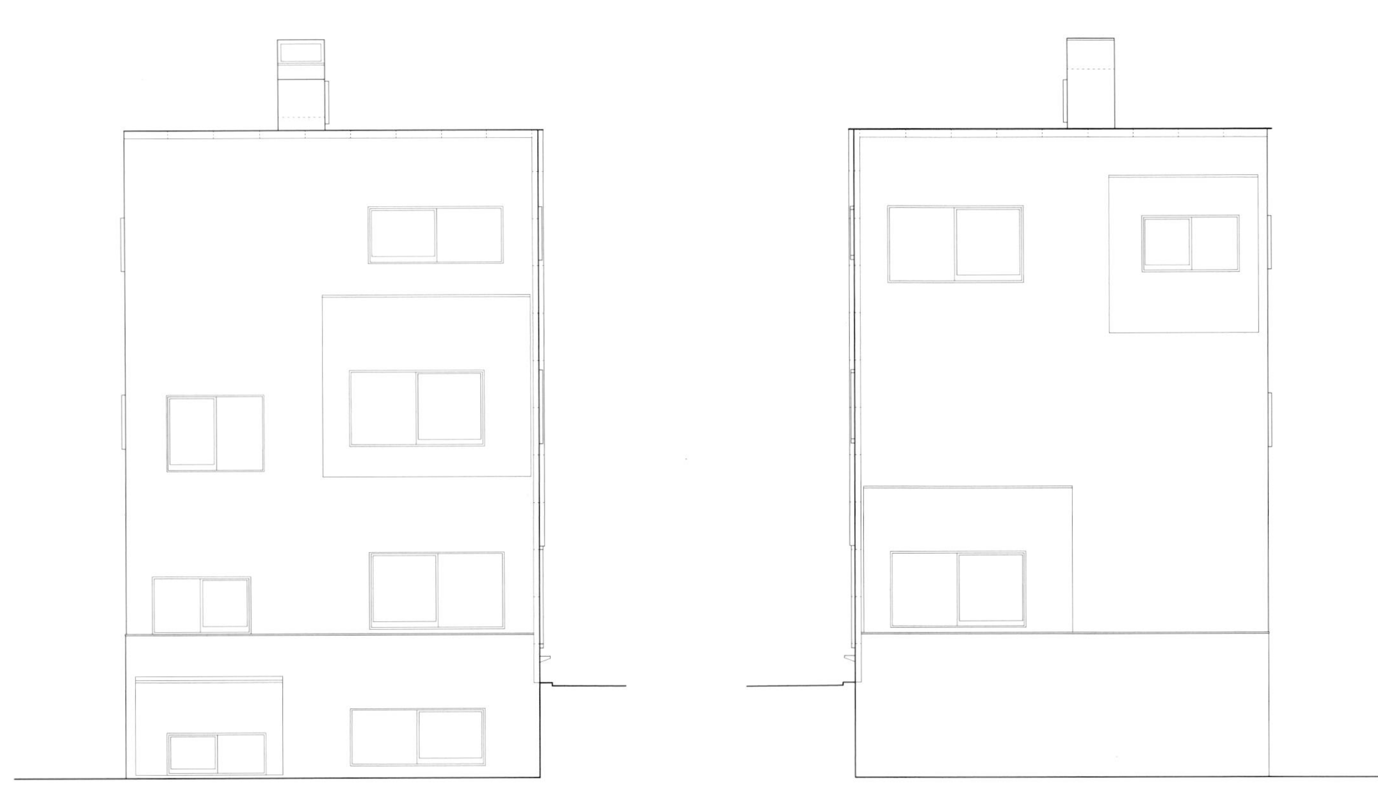
East
West
0
1
2
3m

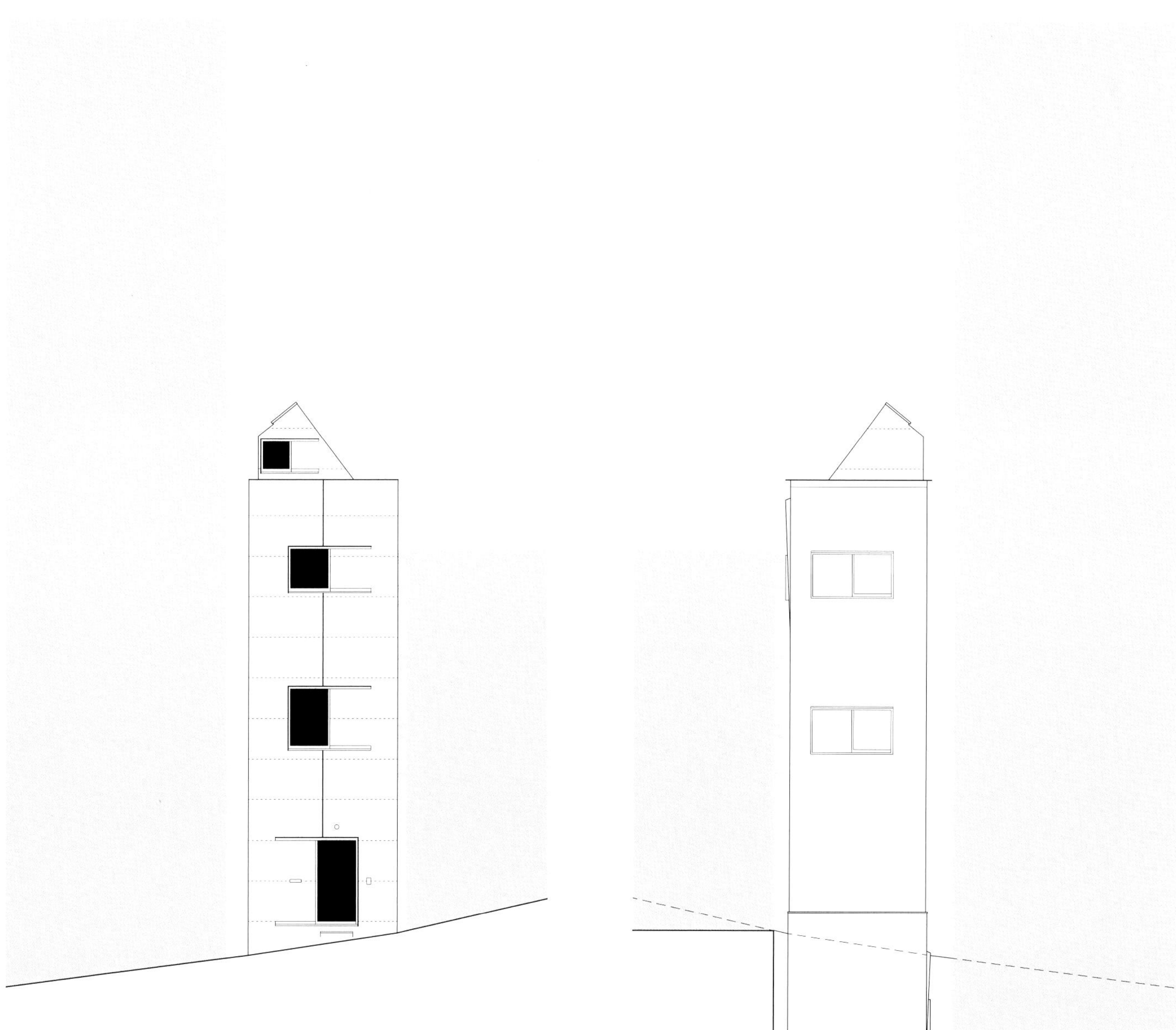

North

South

0 1 2 3m

IN CONVERSATION

Leslie Van Duzer with Reiko Nishio and Hirohito Ono

LVD Welcome Reiko-san and Hiro-san. I would like to start at the very beginning by asking you about the formation of Atelier Nishikata. I am wondering what aspects of your education and early work experience, what confluence of events, led you to start a practice together in 2000.

RN The commission of House in Awaji was the immediate trigger for setting up Atelier Nishikata. It was good timing. First, I had just finished undergraduate architecture studies and was about to go on to graduate school. Plus, Hiro had time. He was involved in art workshops and earthwork projects after finishing one year at a private school of contemporary art. Furthermore, we had a third member, Masaki Mori, who had just quit an architecture firm. So, two freelancers and one grad student started a house project that later became House in Awaji. I worked at an architecture firm for a couple of years before getting into university. There, when I saw the completion of a building I had been in charge of, I felt it was not enough. The building was built properly according to the drawings, but something was missing. Then I thought that if I wanted that "something," though I didn't know what that meant back then, thinking deeply in the design process was essential. So, I went back to school. Hiro also had work experience in several architecture firms. During that period, he had come to a similar conclusion and moved into the contemporary art field. He wanted to think about architecture from a distance for a while.

LVD I am interested in exploring further what exactly you felt was missing from the built work you completed while working in an office.

RN I thought if a project was built, I would gain an experience specific to architecture. But I came to realize that it is hard for a built work to exceed the drawings or models from a spatial point of view and impossible without deliberate thinking in advance. What I expected was a transcendence of the physical realm. So, I decided to go to university and learn from scratch. There was too much I did not know.

LVD Your aspiration to exceed the physical limits of space aligns well with the ambition of many other masterful architects. One thinks for example of Kahn's pursuit of the "immeasurable." It may be also worth noting Mies's description of his own works as "almost nothing." Where do you think your desire to overcome the weight of bricks and mortar comes from?

HO Kahn's "immeasurable" and Mies's "almost nothing" may not have been discussed as the same issue before, but I think it would be very significant in our time and it is an interesting point of view. The two master architects would probably have sought to exceed the physical limits of architecture, but they attempted in the exact opposite way. Simply put, Mies dismantled rooms, and Kahn reinstated "the room." Mies diluted the concept of a window by applying glass walls, but Kahn revived "the window."

RN An answer to your question of where "our aspiration" comes from is not simple, but it is clear that we learn much from the work of architects like Mies and Kahn and Loos, but also from the experience of studying films and paintings. We always discuss those works and what is happening in them.

HO Specifically, House in Awaji gave us the opportunity to explore these ideas. We started thinking about a spatial extension because the site area was so small. Marcel Duchamp once said, "any three-dimensional object, which we see dispassionately, is a projection of something four-dimensional, something we're not familiar with."[1] We thought there was a way to expand three dimensions to four-dimensional space.

LVD So, may I assume that you are interested in the fourth dimension as defined by Einstein as "spacetime," in which the three dimensions of space and one dimension of time are inseparable? Assuming I am on the right track, this makes so much sense. If I had to distinguish your work in one sentence, I would say, it is an architecture that palatably alters our sense of time.

HO Yes, we cannot separate time when thinking about space. The theme of House in Awaji was "One cannot occupy two spaces at the same time." Let's say a person visiting the house for the first time is in the living room. Before that, they entered the music room from the street, stopped by the study, and then are about to head up to the top floor bedroom they have yet to see. At this moment, I expect that the subject experiencing the space of the living room will be recalling the spatial experience of the music room below and imaging the bedroom above, whether consciously or unconsciously. The present in the living room has a wide range of time and space that includes the immediate past in the music room and the immediate future in the bedroom. Our view may be closer to Bergson's duration than Einstein's theory of relativity.

LVD It seems to me this charging of the present with the residue of the past and the anticipation of the future is a strategy you use repeatedly in your other projects as well. I think you tap into the past not only in terms of spatial sequences as you have just described, but also in terms of our memories of architectures past. You challenge our conventional ideas about columns and picture windows and many other things. Can you talk about what is behind these Duchampian moves? Is it always about altering the perception of space at the end of the day?

RN What we always aim for is "releasing perception" or "re-recognition of perception." This is our consistent problem. From this perspective, there might be found something in common with Duchamp's attitude. In any case, in architecture, people perceive only through tangible things,

---

1. Marcel Duchamp and Pierre Cabanne. *Dialogues with Marcel Duchamp.* Translated by Ron Padgett. (New York: Da Capo Press, 1987), 40. Originally published as *Entretiens avec Marcel Duchamp* (Paris: Belfond, 1967).

the "measurable." You cannot exceed physical limits without physical things. That's why the major architectural elements, such as columns and windows, are significant objects.

HO Concerning columns, for example, according to *Architectural Principles in the Age of Humanism* by Rudolf Wittkower, Alberti regarded round columns in a row as the remains of a wall.[2] This audacious definition also applies to modern architecture and we often refer to it when thinking about columns.

RN When we speak about columns, we often talk about those of the Parthenon as well. Hiro has a story about that.

HO About thirty years ago, when I actually saw the columns of the Parthenon up close, I felt they looked hollow rather than solid. I thought there was a space for people inside. It was not easy even for Reiko to see such an image of a hollow column in the Greek temple columns, so I thought it was hard to share with others. But one day, when I was studying Kahn, I found out that he had also mentioned "hollow columns." Moreover, Kahn always brought up the columns of the Greek temple before talking about hollow columns. He did that more than once. I believe the first time was in a letter to Anne Tying.[3] I will not go into the details, but for me, it has long been of interest whether a column is hollow or solid.

RN Recently, we have been researching Mies's high-rise buildings in North America, and one of the motives was the concern about columns. And interestingly, there are "hollow columns" in his buildings as well.

HO Those are the columns on the ground floor of 2400 Lakeview. They are covered with aluminum panels and appear to be the same size. However, when we studied the floor plan in the Mies archives, we realized that some of the columns are not completely filled. What is interesting here is the relationship between three things: a fake column (cladding), a true column (structure), and the space between the two. I think the relationship causes a crack in the normative concept of "column."

LVD I did not know about this particular gap between the structure and the cladding in Mies's Lakeview columns, though by now it is well understood that Mies was no purist when it came to structure. I have long thought honesty in architecture was overstated, not to mention, overrated. In your projects, there is often a gap between what one sees, what is expressed and what is required. Take, for example, your non-structural vaults and canted walls in House in Awaji.

2. Rudolf Wittkower, *Architectural Principles in the Age of Humanism* (New York: Random House, 1965), 34.

3. Alexandra Tyng, *Beginnings: Louis I. Kahn's Philosophy of Architecture* (New York: John Wiley & Sons, 1984), 65–66.

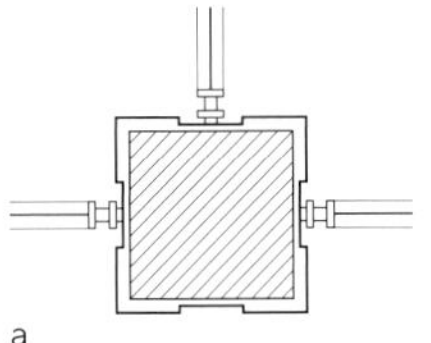

a

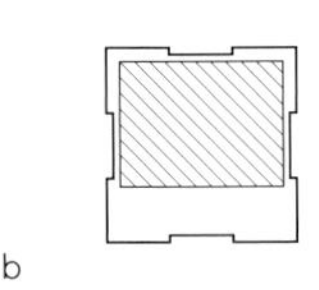

b

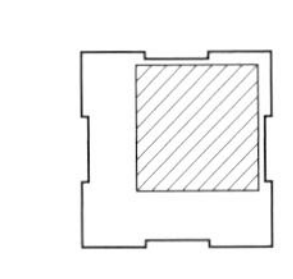

c

2400 Lakeview
Column details

We are talking about the distance between what is required for stability and what is required for expression. Can you elaborate on that?

HO The response to the vaults when House in Awaji was published was split in two. The first response, as we expected, was that this was a false space. That is because the real structure was steel. The other response was, "Aha! We can do it this way. It opened my eyes." One reviewer referred to the ceiling of the auditorium in the Vipuri Library by Alvar Aalto.

RN I thought both responses reflected an obsession with structure and a position that architectural correctness requires expression to follow structure. In our work, sometimes we try to relate them and sometimes not. In House in Awaji, it was the latter case, so we thought about how to create false walls and false ceilings.

HO I guess for Mies, aligning structure and expression was a priority, especially in his clear-span projects such as the Farnsworth House and the New National Gallery, but his attitude was honest even when there was distance between the two. Going back to 2400 Lakeview again, I said earlier that all the columns are the same size in appearance on the ground floor. What is interesting here is that on the residential floors above, the columns are not clad; their reinforced concrete surface is exposed. Mies reveals the trick to us.

Another example is the embedded bookcases in Mies's twin houses in Krefeld, which you and Kent Kleinman analyzed in your book *Mies van der Rohe: The Krefeld Villas.* As you described, the villas appear to have been built of bricks, but the long, embedded bookcases give us a hint that these houses were not built of bricks alone. The Mies archive at MoMA has numerous drawings of the embedded shelves. Mies probably thought about the bookshelves as much as he thought about the windows. I like the villas as converted into museums, but it's disappointing that they buried the shelves.

In House in Awaji, the skylit slit that runs the length of the canted walls reveals that neither the walls nor the vaults are structural. The rooms are clad with Lauan plywood, as are all the sliding doors. When the doors are closed, part of the steel structural frame appears. This subtly tells you that the rooms with the vaults are shaped by thin cladding. We think the disclosure of tricks like this presents an honest attitude to the distance between structure and expression.

LVD It is interesting to me that you are concerned with revealing the truth. You are exposing more than the steel structure; you are exposing your bias towards a well-worn position that honesty has real value in architecture. Can you explain why telling the truth is important to you?

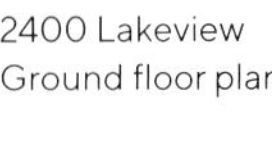
2400 Lakeview
Ground floor plan

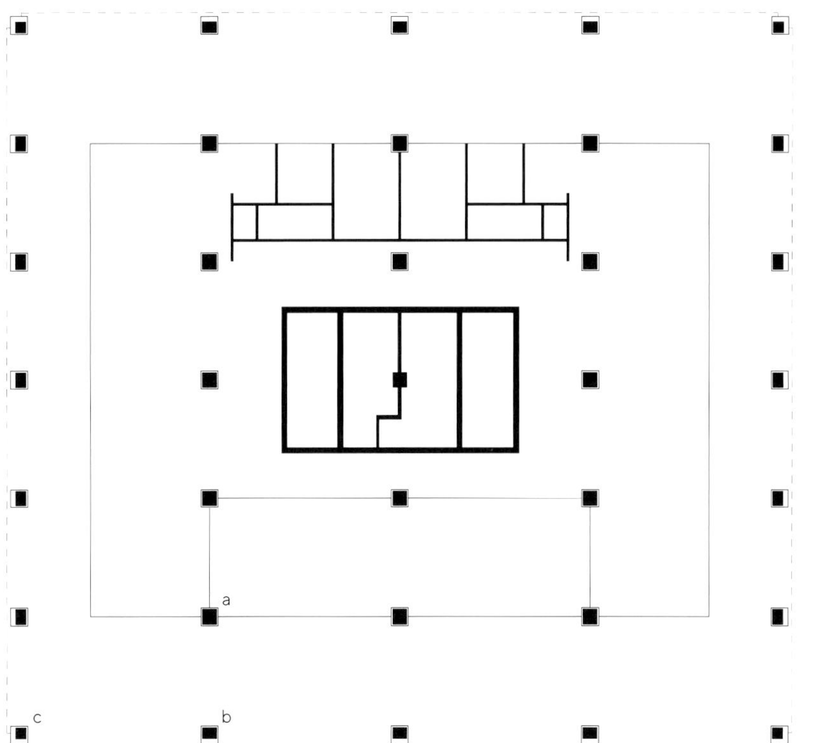

Haus Lange

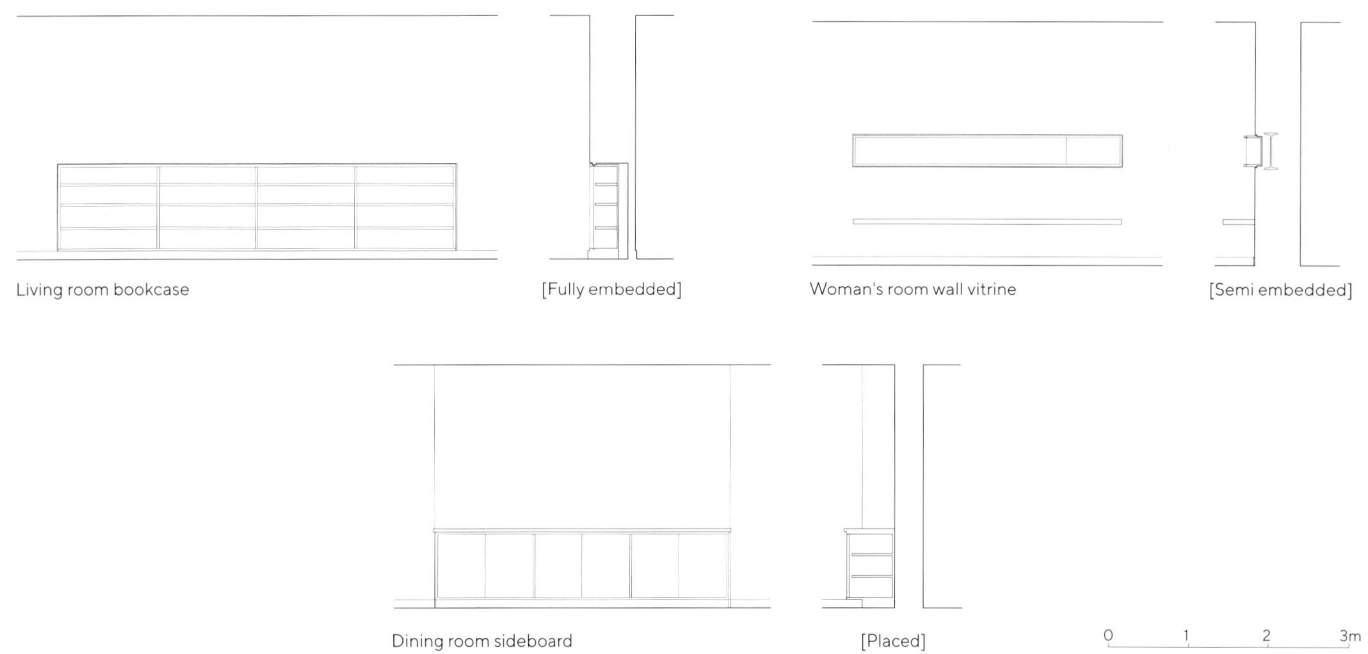

Living room bookcase

[Fully embedded]

Woman's room wall vitrine

[Semi embedded]

Dining room sideboard

[Placed]

HO For us, the important thing is to build up relationships, not to reveal the truth. For example, in the 1980s, Peter Eisenman attempted to interpret Mies, viewing the work as text.[4] That enabled us to analyze architecture independent of formal or metaphorical analyses. I recently realized that my thought overlapped with this "textual analysis." In this view, the questioning of whether the Barcelona Pavilion's cruciform columns are structural elements is suspended. Instead, we consider how they relate to the Pavilion's spatial structure.

RN In Haus Lange and Haus Esters, without the recessed bookshelves, there is only a thesis of brick architecture. By embedding the bookshelves, Mies poses the antithesis: this is not just brick architecture. Generally, this might be called a contradiction, but Hiro calls it "honesty" because the two theses have a strong relationship.

HO Apart from the relationship with the building structure of the brick villas, the bookshelves also have a relationship with the walls. It is necessary to mention that when talking about the bookshelves. Looking at the shelves as furniture, we find there are three types here: fully embedded shelves, half embedded, and not embedded. This relationship between the shelves and the structure is just one of many.

LVD This discussion about the relationship between architectural components—in the case of Mies, columns and cladding, walls and bookshelves, bookshelves and bricks—reminds me of your interest in the relationships between elements in Roberto Rossellini's Neorealist film, *Open City.*

HO In our analysis of *Open City*, we categorized various openings such as lattice windows, closet doors, tunnels, which we call "concrete things" in a film, and carefully examined their relationships. Our analysis shows that these visual relationships are the structural frame that supports the film. We believe that this study has revealed that *Open City* has a "doors story" that is entirely different from the "war story" that has dominated its categorization.

LVD When one realizes the distance between what is required of architecture in terms of structure and enclosure and what is required for expression, one understands the significance of the gap between the two. Thank you both so much for revealing more of the thought behind your work. I know we could go on and on, but instead let's leave the reader wishing there was more.

4. Peter Eisenman, "miMISes READING: does not mean A THING," in *Mies Reconsidered: His Career, Legacy, and Disciples,* organized by John Zukowsky (New York: Rizzoli International Publications, 1986), 86–98.

Roberto Rossellini's *Rome, Open City*, Door Movement

CREDITS

Niki.L / CC BY-SA
photo: 11 (top)

Marc Treib
photo: 11 (middle)

Kunstmuseum Krefeld / Volker Döhne
photo: 11 (bottom)

Ron 't Hart
photo: 14 (top)

Yohan Zerdoun
photo: 14 (middle)

Gaston Wicky
photo: 14 (bottom)

Gigon / Guyer Architects
drawings: 14

Atelier Nishikata
drawings: 8, 18, 21, 30–31, 33, 38–39, 41, 46–47, 49, 56–57, 60, 66–68, 70, 80–81, 84, 86, 89, 100–103, 108–109; photos: 85
(All drawings of Mies's work were delineated based on published documents.)

Reiko Nishio
photos: cover front, cover back, 19 (middle), 20, 23, 32–35, 40, 42–44, 45 (top), 48, 59

Hirohito Ono
photo: 107

Hirohito Ono (drawing) / Yasuyuki Nakamura (design)
drawing: 111

Takeshi Yamagishi
photos: 19 (top and bottom), 24–27, 36 (top), 36–37, 42, 45 (bottom), 50 (right), 52–54, 58, 61–65, 71

Takumi Ota
photos: 6, 69, 73–79, 82, 89–99

Kurashi no Techosha Inc. / Akiko Baba
photos: 29 (top), 36 (bottom)

Shinkenchiku-sha / Taisuke Inatsugu
photos: 2–3, 28, 50 (left), 51

Shinkenchiku-sha / Makoto Yamamori
photo: 84

Shochiku Co., Ltd.
photo: 72

Leslie Van Duzer
photos: 29 (bottom), 55, 104

I would like to extend my gratitude to Jake Anderson and Gordon Goff at ORO for their trust and professionalism; to Pablo Mandel, book designer par excellence, for the great pleasure of working together again; to Karla Forsbeck, Mira Locher, Dr. Duz and my father for reviewing the manuscript; and to Reiko Nishio and Hirohito Ono for the countless contributions they generously made to this book, including many new drawings. Finally, my gratitude and love goes to my brother Eric for levitating me, both literally and figuratively.

—Leslie Van Duzer